GUY DE LA BÉD(

POTTERY IN ROMAN BRITAIN

SHIRE ARCHAEOLOGY

2

Cover photograph
Roman pottery made in Britain, Gaul and the Rhineland and found in Britain.
(Photograph: the author)

British Library Cataloguing in Publication Data:
De la Bédoyère, Guy
Pottery in Roman Britain. – (Shire archaeology)
1. Pottery, Roman – Great Britain
2. Great Britain – Antiquities, Roman
3. Great Britain – Antiquities
4. Great Britain – History – Roman period, 55 B.C.–449 A.D.
I. Title 738.3'09361
ISBN 0 7478 0469 9

Published in 2004 by
SHIRE PUBLICATIONS LTD
Cromwell House, Church Street, Princes Risborough,
Buckinghamshire HP27 9AA, UK.
(Website: www.shirebooks.co.uk)

Series Editor: James Dyer.

Number 79 in the Shire Archaeology series.

ISBN 0 7478 0469 9.

First published 2000; reprinted 2004.

Printed in Great Britain by
CIT Printing Services Ltd, Press Buildings,
Merlins Bridge, Haverfordwest, Pembrokeshire SA61 1XF.

Contents

List of illustrations

Foreword and acknowledgements

The study of Roman pottery is so vast a subject that the literature is colossal, and museum collections even larger. Consequently the study of this bewildering topic has been undertaken by a very large number of people from as far back as the middle of the nineteenth century. Between them they have uncovered a mesmerising array of different vessels, sources, and ways of analysing and understanding them. Despite this, there are some well-established patterns and themes, so the purpose of this work is to provide just an introduction to material which can tell us more than any other find about the Roman period in Britain.

As an historian with an interest in understanding all of Romano-British culture, I regard Roman pottery as one of the most important ingredients in getting to grips with this astonishing period in our history. The Romano-British made, imported and bought pottery, all of which helps reveal their trade routes, their tastes, what they ate, sometimes their names from inscriptions on the vessels, and even their mortal remains, savings and valuables. Fired clay was also used for other purposes as well, and this book includes sections on tiles and ceramic figurines.

I would like to thank Catherine Johns and Don Bailey of the British Museum, Richard Reece, and Ted Connell of the Kent Archaeological Society for their help and advice, and, for his great personal enthusiasm for Roman pottery in the past, the late Christopher St John Breen. Making sense of Roman pottery means that credit is also due to all the other specialists who have worked on this subject for many years, producing pottery reports and discussions of industries, large and small.

All dates are AD unless otherwise stated. All the illustrations and photographs are by myself unless otherwise stated.

Guy de la Bédoyère, Eltham, 2000

Glossary

Appliqué: decorative motifs manufactured (often in a mould) separately and *applied* to the surface of a vessel, using liquid clay as an adhesive, prior to dipping the whole in slip, drying and firing.

Assemblage: a group of pottery vessels found together in the same deposit, such as a grave, and therefore known to have been used at around the same time.

Barbotine: decoration made by trailing liquid clay across the surface of a vessel like icing a cake. Used for simple lines, curves, tendrils and even animals (figures 17, 18).

Beaker: drinking vessel normally with a narrow base, swollen waist decorated with motifs or indentations, and a conical mouth (figures 16, 17, 18, 19, 22, 23).

Burnishing: a polished sheen created by rubbing the finished pot with a tool prior to firing.

Carinated: a marked angle change inwards in a vessel's profile.

Coarse ware: a general term for kitchenwares or goods manufactured for primarily functional, rather than decorative, purposes.

Colour-coat: term used for a **slip**, the colour of which contrasts with the internal fabric of the vessel.

Fabric: term used to describe the material from which a pottery vessel has been made, normally in terms of colour and **temper**.

Flange: protruding ridge around a vessel which is distinct from the rim (for example figure 10p).

Glaze: similar to **slip**, but applied after the vessel has already been fired, followed by refiring, which causes a glass-like effect and a chemical alteration which bonds it with the fabric.

Grog: see **temper**.

Handmade: pottery manufactured by building up clay by hand, either in coils or from a solid block, on a stationary surface.

Mica-dusted: bronze-like finish created with a mica-rich **slip** or mica scattered on to wet clay.

Mortarium: thick and heavy shallow bowl with gritted interior and substantial rim and spout used for grinding food. A characteristically Roman product.

Oxidation: firing technique in which outside air is allowed into the kiln during the process, creating an orange, red or brown fabric. See also **reduction.**

Parchment ware: named for its white- or cream-coloured, sometimes soft, fabric, for example the New Forest coarse parchment ware used to make bowls and mortaria.

Pipe-clay: high-quality white clays used for figurines and since the seventeenth century for clay pipes, hence the term.

Reduction: firing technique in which the kiln is sealed from outside air, creating a grey or black fabric, used normally for kitchenwares.

Rough-cast: application of gritty, sandy specks in the slip, creating a surface like sandpaper.

Rouletting: simple decorative technique created by rotating a tool resembling a cog wheel against a vessel's surface to create parallel rows of narrow vertical lines.

Rustication: application of thickened slip, worked by hand into a scaly, lumpy surface.

Slip: clay, liquidised with water, into which finished pottery vessels were dipped prior to being fired (normally by hand, leaving conspicuous finger marks). See also **colour-coat** and **glaze**.

Temper: inclusions in clay used for pottery, such as fragments of shell ('calcite'), sand, quartz, broken pot ('grog') or stone, to strengthen or fill the fabric. One effect was to minimise shrinkage. Mould-decorated samian, however, needed to shrink so that it could be extracted from the mould. Thus samian, characteristically, has very little prominent temper.

Waster: pot damaged in a kiln where the process has gone wrong, causing burning, collapse, distortion or blistering. Normally found at kiln sites rather than anywhere else.

Wheel-thrown: pottery made on a potter's wheel, leaving distinctive concentric grooves within as the potter's hands draw up the vessel.

1
Roman pottery and the archaeologist

Pliny the Elder, writing in the 70s AD, called earthenware products *inenarribili Terrae benignitate*, 'a kindness of Mother Earth beyond description' (*Natural History* 35.158) and wondered at their limitless applications. Vast quantities of pottery were used in the Roman Empire, reflected in the huge numbers of potsherds found on almost all sites of Roman date (figures 1, 52). Almost indestructible, they are the most common find in every excavation of a Roman settlement.

Potsherds can tell us much about Roman technology, trade and art, and are an important dating tool. But interpreting pottery means classifying it into broad categories such as fine tablewares, like Gaulish samian ware, and ordinary kitchenwares, and then considering the different forms made, the styles of decoration, colours, fabrics and sources. Burials, in which pottery jars were used as cremation urns and other vessels as grave goods, are the most valuable source of contemporary groups of complete pots because they often survive intact, or nearly so (figures 3, 7). Without complete examples to use as models it would sometimes be difficult to know what sort of vessel a broken sherd has come from, and the range of types which existed.

Roman pottery was made throughout the Empire. Distinguishing flagons made in the *Verulamium* (St Albans) area from, say, those imported from Gaul, depends on form and fabric. Colour is important but most basic 'grey' kitchenwares are similar in colour and fabric. Freshly broken sherds can reveal differences in fabric but scientific

1. Pottery from Stonea (Cambridgeshire), including a samian Form 31 dish, various 'hunt cups' and kitchenware jars and a dish. (© Copyright the British Museum.)

2. Samian Form 37 bowl in the style of Cinnamus of Lezoux, *c.*140–80. Dating evidence for his work comes from finds on Britain's northern frontier in the second century. From Plaxtol (Kent).

techniques include taking wafer-thin sections of the fabric and examining them microscopically to identify minerals and other components. This can pin down the source to a specific place. Different inclusions, such as quartz or shell, can mark two similar-looking fabrics as coming from places hundreds of miles apart. The new *National Roman Fabric Reference Collection* (see Tomber and Dore in Further Reading) is unmatched as a detailed guide.

Roman pottery does not date itself. But form and fabric do help provide a basis for a chronology when archaeologists find pottery in an historically dated context, or with dated evidence such as coins or an inscription. The best examples include samian pottery found in fire levels associated with the Boudican Revolt of 60–1 at Colchester, London and *Verulamium* (St Albans), and around 120–5 in the primary building levels on Hadrian's Wall. Samian's distinctive decoration, forms and name-stamps mean that the work of individual potters can be identified in deposits from these events (figures 2, 11, 12). When their work is found elsewhere, it helps date these other sites and also ordinary kitchenwares found in the same assemblages.

But high-value possessions are normally cared for, so identical samian might survive much later elsewhere, perhaps for example being found in a grave with a third-century coin. Such pottery is known as 'residual'. A contemporary parallel could be a modern house destroyed by fire, with the debris including a collection of Victorian crockery as well as coins of the 1990s. Coins themselves are also liable to be residual. So, pottery found securely stratified with a coin of 154 may have been deposited much later (though certainly not before). Unfortunately, there are no third- and fourth-century British sites where deposits can be closely associated with historical events and there is also no equivalent to samian. Consequently, later Roman pottery in Britain is nothing like so well dated.

In spite of these complications, specialists have been able to identify patterns and develop typologies and chronologies of thousands of different pottery forms. But with so many to consider, a simple range of basic classifications (on which this book is based) is essential. Of course, these categories are modern inventions; we rarely have any idea of the names the Romano-British would have used, and the level of prices or availability which will have affected their choice of pottery. To make things worse, early archaeological reports paid little attention to kitchenwares, making comparisons with more recent excavations difficult. Fine wares are also affected. Beakers made in the Rhineland were, for example, often confused with Nene Valley products.

Pottery use in Britain

Before the invasion Roman pottery was mainly available only to tribal aristocrats, making little impact on the archaeological record beyond some rich graves in the south-east (figure 3). Local Iron Age industries existed in southern Britain, making a range of sophisticated wheel-thrown wares but mostly for limited local markets. In much of the north and west pottery was almost unknown, and such communities must have used wood, leather or skin vessels.

As Roman influence spread northwards across Britain pottery usage vastly increased on civilian sites. Pottery found its way into every aspect of daily life. But it would be wrong to assume that the same forms served the same purpose: pottery was extremely flexible. An individual kitchenware jar might have been used for storage, cooking, hoarding coins (figure 46), as a cremation container and, during its lifetime, perhaps for all or none of these.

The types used were mainly Roman during the first century. Specialised Roman forms like mortaria, barely known before 43, became common (figure 30). Roman pottery was therefore both widespread and often broadly consistent in forms but styles also evolved locally, drawing

3. Imported amphorae (Dressel 1) and other pottery goods found in a rich aristocratic grave at Welwyn Garden City (Hertfordshire) and now on display in the British Museum in London.

influences from regional markets and traditions. For example, established British products, such as tankards, were absorbed into some repertoires (figure 39).

Some surviving documents, dated *c*.90–105, from the frontier-zone fort at *Vindolanda* (Northumberland) record the transport of perishables such as fish-sauce and olives, but make little mention of the containers used. One seems to list kitchen equipment, including a pair of *scutulae*, 'platters', and a pair of *trullae*, 'bowls'. The principal force in spreading use of pottery of Roman form throughout Britain was indeed the army. Not only did it import continental pottery for its own use, but also brought in, or attracted, continental potters to the new province. This popularised Roman designs like flagons to indigenous potters who started to produce them also (figure 4). The routes and infrastructure established to satisfy army pottery needs could also supply civilians and carry other goods too.

By the early second century military pottery production had almost ceased as local industries, together with imports, were able to supply

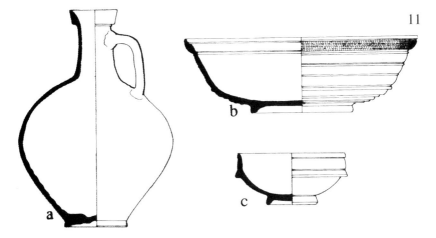

4. Army-made fine wares. Scale about 1/4. **a**. 'Hofheim' flagon from Kingsholm (Gloucestershire). **b**. Imitation samian Form 29 bowl from Kingsholm. **c**. Imitation samian Form 24 cup from Usk (south Wales). (After Darling and Greene.)

not only the army but also the burgeoning civilian market in the developing towns. An example is the potter working a kiln near Upper Caldecote (Bedfordshire) by the early second century and producing red-ware flagons and grey jars. But the army still influenced the market. Fine wares in the north are commonest in major sites like forts or towns such as Corbridge, reflecting their roles as distribution centres. Large numbers of troops were withdrawn from Britain by the governor, Clodius Albinus, to support his unsuccessful bid for power in the civil war of 193–7. The appearance at the end of the second century of north-African-type kitchenware forms (mainly casseroles) in York, but made locally, has been attributed to the arrival of reinforcements from north Africa for the Sixth Legion after 197. This is quite possible but it is as likely that demand also came from other soldiers and local civilians who found the forms convenient, just as Chinese woks have found their way into modern western kitchens.

Although much Romano-British pottery, such as the **Black-Burnished** wares, became important during the first two centuries AD, most better-quality products were imported, particularly Gaulish samian. **Samian** spread across Britain but the industry collapsed during the third century. Established Romano-British industries, like the **Oxfordshire** and **Nene Valley** potteries, took over sections of the market. But they only took regional shares in the market and some, like the **New Forest** industry, had little more than niches. This reflected a trend across the late Empire, perhaps enforced by new laws which made occupations hereditary, towards localised production and distribution.

Another possible explanation is pewter, made from tin and lead. Britain's tin and lead deposits were well worked in the Roman period and pewter-making occurred in many places, such as Nettleton (Wiltshire) and Langton (North Yorkshire), mainly between *c*.250 and *c*.410. Acceptable as a cheap substitute for silver tableware (especially when new), it may have supplanted some of the late fine-ware market. Being infinitely recyclable, pewter is scarce as a site find. Much of what does survive is found in hoards, or deposited in water, probably as votive gifts. This shows how broken pottery's dominance of the archaeological record is partly a function of its durability and uselessness rather than an accurate reflection of what there once was. Kitchenwares were affected too. **Black-Burnished 1** pottery, from the south-west, was a dominant feature of Britain's kitchenware market, almost certainly because of bulk-purchasing by the army, but by the early fourth century its reach had retreated to the south while other industries like **Crambeck** dominated the north during the later fourth century (Map 1).

After the end of Roman rule in the early fifth century Roman-type potting largely ceased in Britain, though isolated instances of manufacture and imports continued. The skill seems to have been widely forgotten during the early 400s. This must have been partly due to the decline of towns, the collapse of organised communications and the disappearance of coinage. Even so, demand for everyday bowls and jugs cannot have vanished, and perhaps wood and leather examples were substituted. In eastern Britain, early Germanic settlers were beginning to introduce distinctive Saxon forms of pottery, usually found in their cemeteries.

Existing Roman pottery might have survived well into post-Roman contexts. There is some evidence that Saxon or Viking immigrants treated it as a valuable curiosity. But it was not until the 1500s and later that Roman pottery was recognised as an antiquity. Antiquarians recorded it and members of institutions like the Royal Society (chartered in 1662) would announce finds of grave groups or jars containing coin hoards. Serious Roman pottery studies did not develop until the nineteenth century when men like Charles Roach Smith (1806–90) and Augustus Pitt-Rivers (1827–1900) made some of the first comprehensive classifications of types and forms.

Manufacture

Potting requires demand, the skill to make it, suitable clay, water, inclusions such as sand for strength, and a means of firing the finished product. Pottery distribution in Britain before the Roman invasion shows that proximity to the Channel played a large part in influencing which tribes had acquired the necessary skills. More sophisticated, wheel-thrown, pottery was more likely to be manufactured in the south-east,

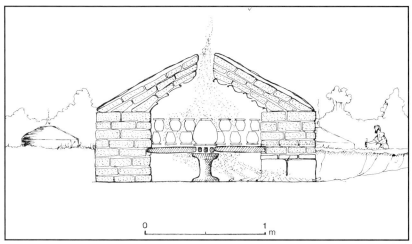

5. Cross-section of a typical Romano-British kiln. A circular depression was dug, together with a lateral stoke-hole. An internal floor suspended the stacked pots above a lower area where the hot gases entered and circulated. The kiln was capped with turf or bricks. If reduced (grey or black) wares were to be made, the roof was sealed and oxygen could not enter. If the pots were to be oxidised, the top was left open. (After Woods.)

and used alongside imported wares.

Some pottery industries of Roman date operated kilns of types which turn up in the ground today (figure 5). Temperature was critical, as was making oxygen available for producing oxidised wares, or keeping it out to fire reduced wares. This depended on the integrity of the superstructure. Failed kilns are often found with the debris including remains of the kiln and also the wasters, providing useful contemporary assemblages of types from a known source, for example the **Black-Burnished 2** vessels found in kilns at Oakleigh Farm, Higham, north Kent.

Much more basic were the bonfire or 'clamp' kilns which existed in pre-Roman Britain. These were little more than insulated bonfires, used to fire kitchenwares. Clamps leave little trace but allowed pottery to be prepared almost wherever and whenever it was needed. The technique remained in use throughout the province all through the period in some industries, such as **Black-Burnished 1**.

Potters often worked in association, building their kilns close together and sharing facilities. Today at **Alice Holt** the mounds of old kilns can be seen within the woodland. Each contains wasters, with the remains of a kiln in the middle. Such sites also yield evidence for pits, water supply, clay stores, workshops and the normal debris of a human occupation site, reflecting how the pottery industry was an integral part of life in Roman Britain. Occasionally it is possible for skilled potters and archaeologists to work in association, making replica Roman pottery and testing kiln techniques and pottery function. These experiments can reveal all sorts of problems about kiln design, suitability of wares for cooking, and so on, which would otherwise never be appreciated.

2
Trade

Before the Roman invasion tribal aristocrats of southern Britain were importing luxury Roman goods in exchange for raw materials. These included fine pottery, and amphorae for their contents like wine and olive-oil (figures 3, 27, 28). Such graves help show that trading networks were well established by the first century BC, even if the quantity was tiny compared to the Roman period. Pliny the Elder tells us about the Empire-wide reputation enjoyed by some wares which were 'so distinguished' they were transported 'this way and that over land and sea' (*Natural History* 35.161).

Although only pottery usually survives, these trade routes must also have carried perishable goods. During the four centuries or so of Roman occupation pottery manufacture and usage in Britain reached levels that would not be matched again for more than a thousand years.

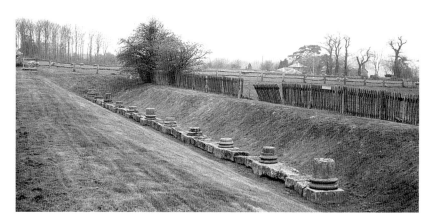

6. The Wroxeter forum colonnade. (Above) The site today. (Below) Plan showing where stacks of new samian bowls were scattered during the late-second-century fire. (After Atkinson.)

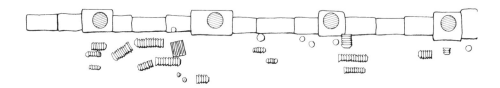

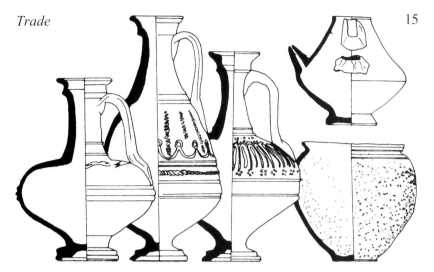

7. Colchester grave group. Scale about 1/3. Fine wares from a grave found about 600 metres south-west of the colony at Colchester in 1866: (left to right) three Central Gaulish lead-glazed ware flagons; (above) feeding bottle; (below) Lyon ware rough-cast beaker. (After Greene.)

Pottery traders

Little is known about how pottery manufacture and its transportation were organised. Evidence of certain wares, like **Lyon** ware, or olive-oil amphorae, which tend to turn up at forts, suggests that traders and contracts specialised in civilian or military trade. Towns and forts near the east coast, like Colchester and York, were well placed to enjoy imported goods (figure 7).

An undated altar from by the mouth of the Scheldt at Domburg in Holland was dedicated to a local goddess called Nehalennia, thanking her for 'merchandise kept safe' by one Marcus Secund(inius?) Silvanus. He calls himself *negotiator cretarius Britannicianus*, normally interpreted as 'trader in bowls with Britain'. The exact meaning here of *cretarius*, a rare word, is uncertain. It may refer to a specific type of bowl, *crater*, used for mixing wine and water, or more generally to earthenware products made from light-coloured or whitish clay, *cretae*. The altar, together with many other dedications to the goddess found there, probably marks a gift after a successful voyage across the North Sea, but whether he was shipping goods into, or out of, Britain is unknown.

The Wroxeter forum

Traders like Silvanus were probably dealing only in bulk consignments. Off the north coast of Kent is a barely submerged obstacle called the 'Pudding Pan Rock'. It earned its name when fishermen started dredging what they called 'pudding pans' from the sea-bed nearby. These were, in fact, samian dishes and bowls and probably represent one or more bulk shipments of samian being brought from Gaul to Britain but wrecked in this hazardous location. Traders had good reason to thank their favourite god or goddess for a successful trip across these dangerous waters.

Once the consignment was in Britain it will have been sold on to wholesalers at ports in Britain, or perhaps their agents will have sold them at auction to local distributors. During the excavation of the forum at Wroxeter (Shropshire), it was discovered that there had been a disastrous fire in the late second century. During the clearing up, wrecked stalls and their goods were buried under a new surface. One trader was selling Gaulish samian (which helped date the fire) alongside Romano-British mortaria and whetstones. The samian was found still stacked (figure 6), and name-stamps show they had already been mixed up from a variety of different workshops.

The spread of wares

Within Britain itself, pottery made in the island could be moved over considerable distances. During the fourth century, Alice Holt kitchenwares dominated south-east Britain but with a marked bias to

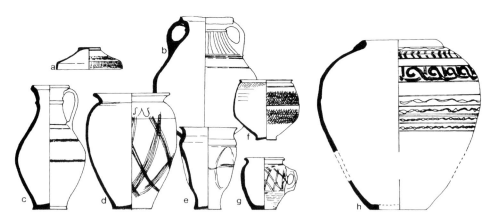

8. Pottery (selected) from the villa at Lullingstone (Kent). Scale about 1/8 (except **h**). **a**. Nene Valley 'Castor Box' lid, unstratified. **b**. Much Hadham oxidised two-handled necked jar, *c*.180–400. **c**. Oxfordshire red-brown colour-coated angular-lipped flagon from a post-286 context. **d**. Black-Burnished 2 jar, with graffito S∧S, second century. **e**. Grey-slipped ware indented beaker from north Kent, late second to mid third century(?). **f**. Colchester rouletted beaker found with Hadrianic samian. **g**. Kentish grog-tempered mug, *c*.175–250. **h**. Alice Holt grey-slipped storage jar, *c*.270+, height about 75 cm. (After Pollard.) See Map 1 for sources.

places accessible by river from the kilns. Long before, the military market on the northern frontier in the second century had relied on the Black-Burnished kitchenwares of south-west Britain and the Thames estuary (see Chapter 6). Widespread in their own areas of production, they also turn up along the northern frontier in substantial quantities. This makes it likely they were shipped from production areas directly to the north. What we cannot find out though is whether they were the main reason for the trade, or whether they were space-fillers in ships loaded with other goods. Such pots were of low intrinsic value and it seems, by our standards, improbable that so much trouble would be devoted to transporting cheap goods so far.

Romano-British consumers probably had little idea where most of their day-to-day pottery came from. Pottery from the well-known villa at Lullingstone (Kent) has been closely studied, showing that the various owners used wares from across central and southern Britain, as well as imported goods (figure 8).

3
Samian ware

Samian was called after pottery from the island of Samos and the Latin verb *samiare*, 'to polish'. The name was used for similar goods from elsewhere, much as we use the word 'china' to describe fine pottery today. Pliny the Elder said it was 'praised for its suitability for dining' (*Natural History* 35.160).

Samian is now used to refer to the red-slip tableware products of Gaul. They are almost all distinguished by pink-red or orange fabrics and a deep glossy red slip, though some potters created 'black samian'. Vessels were wheel-thrown and, when finished, dipped by hand into the slip (leaving fingerprints) before being fired in large kilns, often shared by many potters. Samian was valued enough to be skilfully repaired (figure 13). In Britain samian turns up most in forts and towns, but it is also found in modest graves and remote settlements, showing that red-gloss tableware was a fashion which almost everyone aspired to own, according to means.

Arretine ware, made in northern Italy and in Gaul, was the first major red-slip pottery to appear in the western provinces. Some found its way to the late Iron Age chieftains of southern Britain but in the years following the conquest Arretine gave way to the **South Gaulish** samian (map 2; figure 9) which during the first century AD entered Britain in unprecedented amounts. Samian soon came to dominate the whole fine-ware market, much coming from **La Graufesenque**. Graffiti on samian found at the production sites record kiln-loads in tens of thousands of vessels. Despite the quantities, demand outstripped supply. Potters in Britain and in Gaul produced imitation samian forms which were also

9. South Gaulish Form 29 samian bowl stamped by Celadus. About 55–70. (© Copyright the British Museum.)

probably cheaper. The army had access to a broader range of genuine samian forms than those available to contemporary civilian markets. Pottery industries close to most legionary bases of the first and early second centuries, such as Usk and Gloucester, and perhaps established by the army, also produced imitation samian (figure 4).

By around 100 the **Central Gaulish** potters of **Les Martres-de-Veyre** seem to have taken over but by *c*.120–5 the nearby factories at **Lezoux** were firmly in control of the market. By *c*.190–210 the Central Gaulish industry was in decline. Factories in East Gaul, such as **Rheinzabern**,

10. Plain samian forms. Scale about 1/5. None postdates the first few decades of the third century. Unless otherwise specified the Form number is in the sequence classified by Dragendorff. **a**. Form 24/25, *c*.43–65. **b**. Form 27, *c*.50–170. **c**. Form 33 (early), first century. **d**. Form 33 (late), second century. **e**. Curle Form 11, *c*.70–140. **f–g**. Form 35 cup and Form 36 dish, first and second centuries. **h**. Form 18, *c*.50–100. **i**. Form 31, *c*.125+. **j**. Form 31R (with rouletted circle inside, see figure 11, below). **k**. Form 15/17, first century. **l**. Form 79, *c*.160+. **m**. Ritterling Form 13 inkwell, first and second centuries. **n**. Curle Form 15, second century. **o**. Curle Form 23, *c*.70+. **p**. Form 38 (widely imitated by Oxfordshire and other industries), *c*.125+. **q**. Curle Form 21, *c*.150+. **r**. Form 45, *c*.170+. **s**. Form 44, *c*.125+. **t**. Form 81, *c*.120–70. **u**. Form 40, *c*.150+.

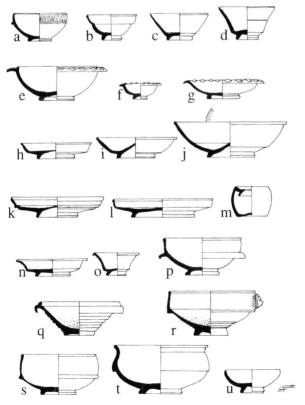

filled the gap but with often inferior products. By around 230 the industry was effectively dead and other, more localised, production centres took over. However, some samian may have continued to reach Britain for a few years while existing pottery will have continued in use.

Plain samian

Undecorated samian forms, such as bowls, dishes and cups, were produced to fairly consistent shapes and standards in huge numbers (figure 10). Despite the broad range of types only a few dominated the market, reflected in site finds. These are principally Form 27 and 33 cups, Form 18, 18/31 and 31 dishes, and Form 38 bowls. In the Wroxeter forum gutter find, for example, 160 out of 197 plain bowls were Form 31 alone (figure 6). Less common finds include the Form 45 mortarium (with lion's head spout), inkwells and jugs.

Many plain samian forms were stamped by their makers. The products of individual workshops can be tracked across much of western Europe (figure 11). Of course only one part of the dish or cup carries the stamp. Wall, base and rim sherds are not of great use apart from where enough survives to show that the example belonged to a variant of a form which is known to belong to a particular period. Samian stamps usually adopt a standard formula. The letters OF indicate *officina*, or 'workshop', thus OF.CALVI, 'the workshop of Calvus'. F indicates *fecit*, 'made',

11. Plain samian name-stamps. (Top) Interior base of a Central Gaulish samian Form 33 cup stamped SENNIVSF, *Sennius fecit*, 'Sennius made this', *c.*120–50. (Below) Interior base of a Central Gaulish samian Form 31R dish with the stamp CINTVSMIX, where X probably represents MA, for *manu*, 'by the hand of Cintusmus', *c.*160–80. Both from Billingsgate, London.

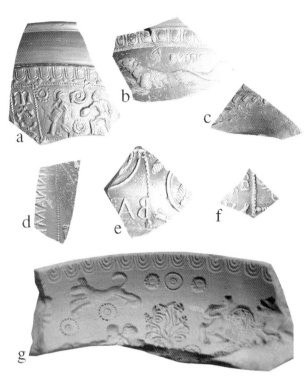

12. Decorated samian manufacturers. Several name-stamps were 'the right way round' on the mould and thus appear backwards on the finished bowls. **a.** Unsigned but the unmistakeable design and motifs used by Drusus I of Les Martres-de-Veyre, *c.*100–25. **b.** Butrio of Lezoux, *c.*120–40. **c.** Paterclus of Lezoux, *c.*125–50. **d.** Cinnamus of Lezoux, *c.*140–80 (see also figure 2). **e.** Banuus of Lezoux, *c.*160–200. **f.** Doeccus of Lezoux, *c.*165–200 (see also figure 13). **g.** Part of a Form 37 mould from the samian kiln site at Colchester featuring an animal chase.

thus SENNIVS.F means 'Sennius made [this dish]' (figure 11). MA is short for *manu*, 'by the hand', thus RVFFI.MA means 'by the hand of Ruffus'.

Decorated samian

Certain samian forms were embellished with barbotine, appliqué, rouletted or incised decoration. Apart from the Form 35 cup and Form 36 dish with their barbotine-decorated rims, these styles are uncommon and cannot be attributed to individual manufacturers.

Mould-decorated samian was much more common. To make it, decorative details such as leaves, figures and abstract motifs were pressed into a layout of panels and zones on a clay mould while it was still soft (figure 12g). Sometimes the mould was signed by hand, or stamped within the decoration or below it. During the period *c.*43–75 the dominant mould-decorated bowl was Form 29, distinguished by its rouletted rim and carinated profile (figure 9). The best-known is the Form 37 hemispherical bowl which took over from *c.*75 on (figure 2), or the similar, but vertically sided, Form 30.

Once the mould was fired it was ready for use, or for sale on to another potter. To make a Form 37 bowl, clay was pressed into the mould, set on a wheel, and a bowl drawn up together with a plain rim above the mould. Once the bowl was dry, shrinkage enabled its removal, leaving the mould to be used again. A base was then applied to the bowl, which was dipped in slip, dried, and stacked in the kiln with dozens of others. Kiln wasters show this was the case, while excavated examples often show traces of grit inside where another bowl had once sat in the kiln.

Many decorated-bowl makers are known. The Cinnamus factory of Central Gaul, in operation between about 140 and 180, dominated the market, and products turn up across Britain, from Kent (figure 2) to forts on the northern frontier. It is this area with its dated periods of activity, such as Hadrian's Wall, built *c.*122, and the Antonine Wall, built *c.*140, which provides much evidence for when some of these potters were active. Individual decorative motifs make it possible to identify products of specific factories. The work of Drusus I (*c.*100–25) can be easily recognised because of his very personal style (figure 12a).

It is difficult to know how much the decoration meant to customers. Being in the lower registers, designs are sometimes difficult to see, but the striking colour, distinctive forms and technical achievement of mass-produced quality goods must have made decorated samian one of the most conspicuous 'Roman' goods available in Britain. Not only that, but the images used in decorated samian widely publicised Roman styles, motifs and figures such as gladiators (figure 12a), personalities from myth, and even exotic wild animals (figure 13). Curiously, the many attempts at imitating samian (see below, and Chapter 4) are characterised by never reproducing, except at Colchester, impressed-mould decoration, as if this was a technique the potters of Oxfordshire and other places never quite understood.

Romano-British samian

At least three, ill-fated, attempts were made to produce samian in Britain. Around 160 a group of potters set up at **Colchester**, making samian closely resembling East Gaulish versions. The location makes it likely they had decided to try and cut out the risky sea voyage and make their goods where they would be bought. Their kiln site, workshops and other debris have been excavated, yielding pieces of several hundred Form 37 moulds alone (figure 12g).

If this sounds like a good idea, it turned out not be. Colchester samian ought to have been cheaper. But the clay was inferior and the products may have been regarded as unfashionable. As a prestige product, some of samian's appeal may have been its cost. Alternatively, it is just as

13. Decorated samian styles. (Clockwise from top left) Central Gaulish Form 78 conical cup, a rare form, with figured scene and name-stamp BVTRIO of Lezoux (see also figure 12b), *c.*120–40, from London. Central Gaulish Form 37 sherd in the style of Servus I, mid second century; the design is a continuous wavy line around leaf designs and a pair of figures; from London. Central Gaulish Form 37 bowl in the typical panelled and roundel style of Doeccus of Lezoux, *c.*165–200; note the lead-rivet repair on the right; from Hayton (North Yorkshire).

possible that existing traders exploited political contacts to confound the Colchester potters' attempts to break into the market.

But Colchester samian made almost no impact on the Romano-British market and it disappeared, the kilns and equipment being abandoned. The same applies to the unknown Nene Valley potter who produced moulds between about 160 and 200 for Form 37 bowls, with decoration incised, rather than impressed, into the moulds. Known only from a handful of his products found in a Nene Valley kiln, he seems perhaps to have made just one, unsuccessful, attempt to take a share of this lucrative market. There was also the so-called **Aldgate-Pulborough** potter whose rare products, probably made in London, were badly made. Not only does he seem to have been unable to fire his bowls properly but they are covered with gouges and scratches.

Samian supply

Being well dated and identifiable, samian has been more closely studied than some other classes of Roman pottery. One phenomenon that has been identified is erratic supply. First-century samian from South Gaul seems to have been imported in much higher quantities than the Central Gaulish products of the second century, and East Gaulish was never more than a small part of the British market.

There seems to have been a steady decline in samian supply during the second century. This would help explain the Colchester and Nene Valley enterprises but the decline was followed by the disappearance of Gaulish samian by the first few decades of the third century. The reasons are unknown but the Battle of Lyons in 197, which settled a civil war, may have disrupted the region. Other, Romano-British, pottery industries, many of which had been active for more than a century, were now free to fill the tableware gap. Even so, it is likely that many individual samian bowls or dishes remained in use for a very long time and perhaps continued to stimulate production of similar types by Romano-British fine-ware industries.

4
Other tablewares

Samian dominated the tableware market in the western Empire during
the first two centuries AD, but never monopolised it. Other fine-ware
industries were producing distinctive goods like cups, goblets and
flagons. Many other wares were imported, largely because of the military
market (map 2). Romano-British potteries also developed, often
producing utilitarian kitchenwares alongside fine wares (map 1). The
Oxfordshire industry, for example, produced pots of almost every class
though nothing is known about how this was organised and whether the
same potters were responsible. The most popular forms included beakers,
and also a range of dishes and bowls which resembled samian products.
This conservatism, exhibited over several centuries, is as remarkable as
the diversity of sources. Unlike the samian industries, these fine-ware
potters scarcely ever used name-stamps and consequently we can never
know as much about them or date their products as closely.

Imported tablewares
   Central Gaulish glazed wares were used across northern Gaul and
Britain from the time of the conquest up to the early 70s (figure 7).
Compared to samian the quantities are tiny. Forms include single-handled
jugs or flagons, a version of the samian Form 29 bowl, jars and two-
handled goblets or cups which resembled glass, gold and silver models.
Goblets and cups were used for wine-drinking, while the later appearance
of beakers from other industries is probably due to a more widespread
provincial taste for beers. Goblets and cups were derived from silver
and gold models and, like the flagons and Form 29 type bowl, were
partly manufactured in moulds to create simple decorative schemes
based on patterns of lines, arches and leaves. In other cases, motifs were
applied to finished vessels. The lead-glaze makes these products
distinctive. Almost always of a hue somewhere between yellow and
green, the effect is similar to some medieval wares.
   Gallo-Belgic wares were amongst the most important imported fine
wares from the late first century BC up to about 75, making a substantial
impact on the pottery market of southern, eastern and central Britain but
mainly associated with civilian settlements (figure 14). Of the variants,
Terra rubra was produced near Rheims in a variety of fabrics and
slips, almost all of which offered variants on orange and red in a range
of dishes, cups and beakers, many of which clearly borrowed from
Arretine and samian forms. **Terra nigra** was made in the same area and
also around Trier, producing a similar range of vessels but in grey

26

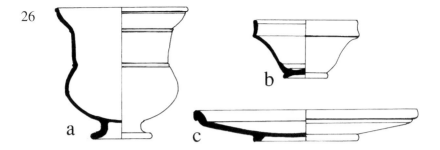

14. Gallo-Belgic wares. Scale about 1/5. **a**. Gallo-Belgic butt-beaker, mid to late first century. **b**. Gallo-Belgic cup emulating an Arretine type, mid to late first century. **c**. Gallo-Belgic platter emulating samian Forms 15 and 17, mid to late first century. (After Hawkes and Hull, and Rigby.)

fabrics and grey to dark-grey or black slips. **Eggshell terra nigra** was very thin and delicate, as the name suggests, and is best known for a beaker shaped like a much larger cooking jar, and a carinated beaker. The use of very thin walls may have been an attempt to emulate the tactile quality of precious-metal wares. The area may also have been the source of some mica-dusted goods (see below).

Another regional Gaulish product which found a first-century British market was **Lyon** ware, typically as a range of rough-cast, barbotine, scaled or stamped hemispherical cups. Although produced in Central Gaul, continental distribution is biased to East Gaul and along the Rhine, which probably reflects trade routes associated with the army and is borne out by its distribution mainly on military sites in Britain.

African red slip ware was manufactured in an extensive variety of dishes, bowls and cups, many of which emulated samian forms (figure 15). Also capitalising on the taste for red tableware, it lasted considerably longer than any other source, which makes the demise of samian all the more curious. Despite failing to capture much of the Gaulish market,

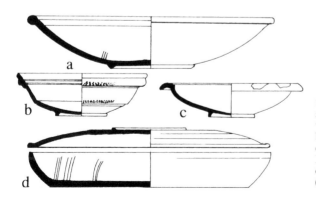

15. Red-slip wares. Scale about 1/5. **a–c**. African red slip ware dishes and bowls. Late second century on. **d**. Pompeian-Red ware dish with lid, c.50–80. (After Peacock.)

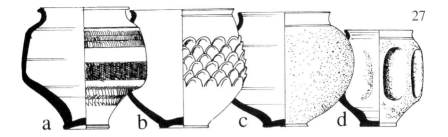

16. Colour-coated beakers from the Lower Rhineland / Cologne area with different decorative styles. Scale about 1/5. **a.** Rouletted. **b.** Scaling. **c.** Rough-cast. **d.** Rough-cast. Some types resemble Gaulish, Colchester and Nene Valley products. Second to early third century. See also figure 17. (After various sources.)

African red-slip goods spread around the Mediterranean, across Italy and up through the Rhineland to appear over much of Britain from the second through to the fourth century, and reappearing as an import in the sixth century. Much rarer is **Egyptian red slip** ware, widespread in its own region, but known in Britain only from one stratified sherd found in an early-fourth-century context in London.

Pompeian-Red ware is named for its deep red colour, resembling the wall-paint best known at Pompeii. Produced mainly as wide shallow dishes and lids in southern Italy and southern Gaul, it, too, belonged to the broader red-slipped ware tradition (figure 15). The products reached a number of sites in Britain between *c.*50 and 75, but only in small quantities, as did **Spanish colour-coated** ware, made in Baetica *c.*50–80. Distribution suggests it relied on coastal shipping traffic around Spain and Gaul to enter northern Europe through the river system and then down the Rhine across to Britain. Responsible for a small range of cups and beakers with an orange-brown slip, the industry was supplying a specialist market which, in Britain, was served to a much greater extent by more local industries.

At around the time Central Gaulish glazed ware was disappearing, **Lower Rhineland colour-coated** ware started to enter the British market (figure 16). It was certainly made at Cologne, the source of numerous other products shipped to Britain. This probably helped disperse it across the new province, though distribution is biased to the south-east from *c.*80 right up to *c.*250. The most popular, and recognisable, products were beakers with their distinctive white fabric and the thin dark-brown or even blue-black slip, easily worn away to expose the fabric. These are characterised by their wide mouths, neat small angular rims, and conical bases tapering to a small circular pedestal. Decoration includes barbotine decoration animal chases (figures 17, 18), and rough-cast (which aided grip). Other variants include bands of rouletting and scaling, and vertical indentations around the beaker. They are difficult to distinguish from Nene Valley products, but this at least shows they must have been serving the same markets.

Also active during the same period, but on a much smaller scale, was the **North Gaulish grey** ware industry. Producing a variety of elegant forms, including a range of beakers and bowls, in the area around Calais, it seems to have impacted only on the extreme south-east of Britain, with scattered examples up the east coast. Decoration was restricted to rouletting, though the dark-grey surface will have made them resemble the Rhineland colour-coated beakers (above). But the vessel form of the beakers is generally different, with their elongated necks and bulbous bodies.

Between *c*.150 and 210 **Central Gaulish black-slipped** ware, made

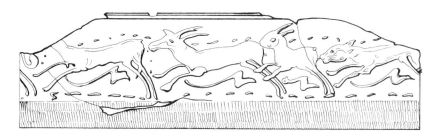

17. Hunt cup frieze on a Lower Rhineland / Cologne black-slipped beaker found at the New Fresh Wharf, London. Late second, early third century. See also figure 16.

18. Beaker designs. (Left) Fragment of a Lower Rhineland beaker depicting a hare. See also figure 17. (Right) Sherd from a Nene Valley beaker showing a hunter.

in and around the Central Gaulish samian industry, shared the market for elegant dark-colour-coated cups and beakers (figure 19). This is interesting because its distribution, mainly northern Gaul and Britain, suggests the forms appealed to a more regional market despite being produced by an area which supplied a much wider zone with samian products. Not surprisingly, fabrics and even some forms are more or less the same as Central Gaulish samian; in this respect it could strictly be seen as a variant of black samian (see Chapter 3). Decoration is normally rouletting or barbotine.

Trier black-slipped ware captured the same British market as the Central Gaulish version. Made at Trier, it was shipped out across the North Sea, as well as capturing a continental market in the region of production. A similar range of beakers was produced but these can be distinguished by the darker red fabric, and the more extravagantly decorated examples featured white trailed motifs over the dark slip, sometimes as letters spelling out drinking exhortations, such as BIBE, 'drink!' (figure 19f).

During the third century and beyond, Romano-British producers were responsible for servicing mainly the tableware market. Some continental products still found their way into Britain as well as the longer-lived

19. Black-slipped wares. Scale about 1/5. **a–c**. Central Gaulish black-slipped wares with barbotine and rouletted decoration. The ease with which sources of these products can be confused is evident by comparing **b** with figure 22e. *c.*150–200. **d–f**. Trier black-slipped ware, with **f** bearing white painted decoration and the motto DA MERVM, 'serve unmixed wine'. (After various sources.)

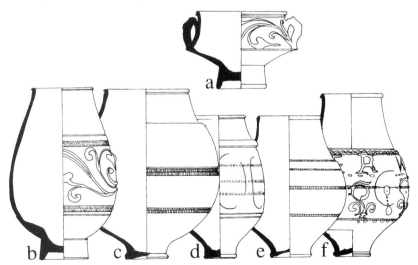

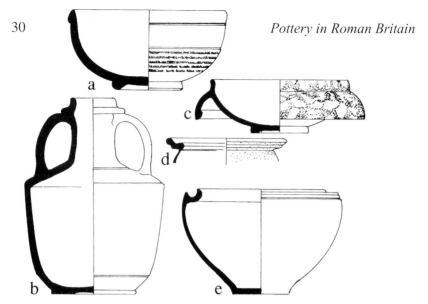

20. Late Roman imported wares. Scale about 1/5. **a**. Argonne ware emulating samian Form 37 with roller-stamp decoration. Fourth century. **b**. Rhineland or German marble ware two-handled flagon. Mid third to fourth century. **c**. *Céramique à l'éponge* flanged bowl, exaggerating samian Form 38, and with characteristic sponged decorative effect. Fourth century. **d**. Mayen ware lid-seated jar. Early to mid third century. **e**. Mayen internal flange bowl perhaps designed for taking a lid. Fourth century. (After various sources.)

African red slip products (see above) but in tiny amounts (figure 20). **Argonne** ware, for example, manifested mostly as an anodyne version of the samian Form 37 bowl, decorated only with rouletting and in a characteristic dull orange fabric and slip, spread widely across northern Gaul but only impacted on south-east and central Britain between *c*.270 and 410. **Céramique à l'éponge**, made in western Gaul, entered southern Britain throughout the fourth century, mainly as a large bowl similar to samian Form 45, and a hook-flanged bowl resembling samian Form 38 (figure 20c). With a characteristically yellow-brown slip and mottled finish, the appearance resembles a home-made marbling effect.

Romano-British tablewares

Not surprisingly, tableware industries first developed in the south-east. Some **mica-dusted** wares were being made by the late first century, modelled on continental originals. The product, which resembles new bronze, was an effective way of creating cheap goods with a quality appearance and is closely associated with the army.

By the later first century so-called **London** ware appeared, with sources probably scattered across the London area, Kent (for example at **Upchurch**), and up into East Anglia, perhaps as far as the **Nene Valley**.

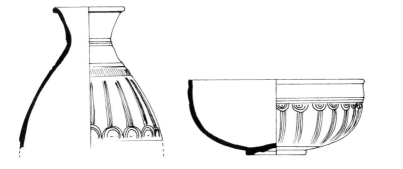

21. 'London' ware. Scale about 1/5. (Left) Narrow-necked jar with incised and stamped decoration. (Right) Bowl emulating samian Form 37. Both late first, early second century. (After Marsh.)

Although made of grey or black fabric, many of the types were modelled on samian Forms 29 and 37 but with only the most cursory decoration, using rouletting, incising and stamps (figure 21). These lasted on into the middle of the second century, coinciding with the decline in samian supply. More elaborate, and with better-executed decoration, but essentially part of the same tradition was **London-Essex stamped** ware, produced in the Hadham area from *c*.80 to *c*.130. This is represented mainly by an elegant pedestal bowl form with rings of zoned stamped decoration using concentric circle motifs, lines and rouletting.

Various other industries also developed in the south-east, some for example producing the so-called 'poppy-head' beakers with their characteristic globular bodies, everted rims and panels of black dots over a grey polished surface. These were made at places like **Upchurch** on the Thames estuary and at **Highgate Wood**. They appeared from *c*.70 and lasted on into the third century though the Highgate production had died out not long after *c*.160.

South-East English glazed ware, apparently produced in Staines (an important river crossing on the route west), made some impact in the south-east between *c*.75 and 120. Resembling earlier glazed imports in some respects and certainly in colour, albeit darker, the wares borrowed from small samian forms, mainly Forms 67 and 78.

Colchester colour-coated wares developed as London wares declined and lasted until *c*.250; rough-cast, rouletted, and indented beakers were produced, of types broadly similar to those being made in the Lower Rhineland (figure 16). It is likely they were made by potters who moved across the North Sea, like the migrating samian potters (see Chapter 3). Potters at **South Carlton** (Lincolnshire) produced mortaria for the north and the Antonine Wall between *c*.140 and 170 but supplemented production with colour-coated beakers for the same market.

Colchester products began to disappear from the market at the same time as other principal Romano-British tableware industries were

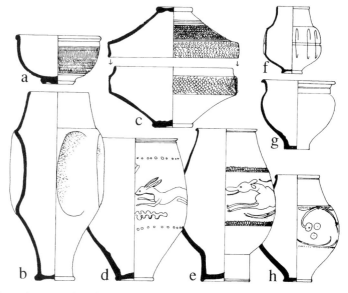

22. Nene Valley, colour-coated products (except g). Scale about 1/5. **a.** Bowl with rouletted decoration emulating samian Form 37, *c.*270–350. **b.** Indented beaker. **c.** 'Castor Box' (bowl and lid). **d.** 'Hunt cup', *c.*170–230. **e.** 'Hunt cup' with a base resembling Central Gaulish products, *c.*200–30. **f.** 'Slit-folded' beaker, fourth century? **g.** Wide-mouthed grey-ware jar, third century. **h.** Barbotine-decorated beaker, *c.*170–200. Dates very approximate. (After various sources, including Howe, Mackreth, Perrin and Swan.)

becoming well established. The **Nene Valley colour-coated** industry was lively enough to contribute to the development of a town at Water Newton (*Durobrivae*) in Cambridgeshire. Potting had first started up in the area when the army passed through during the mid first century. A century later a colossal range of beakers was produced here, using Rhineland examples as models, perhaps made by migrant potters, but two-handled flagons, bowls modelled on samian forms (including one attempt to produce moulded decoration) and dishes were also made, as well as the so-called 'Castor Box', a conical bowl with tapered base and a lid of similar proportions and size (figure 22). The styling and colour of the products make them difficult to distinguish from continental examples but the fabric and slip have a more orange or

23. Nene Valley colour-coated beaker with an erotic scene. These are less common than hunt scenes or animal chases but certainly not unusual. Late second, early third century. Height about 12.5 cm.

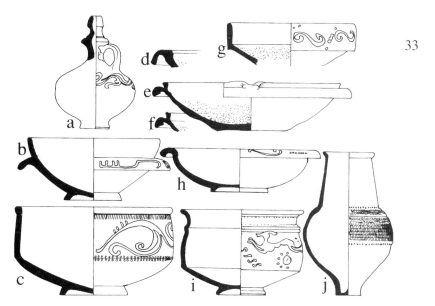

24. Oxfordshire products. Scale about 1/5. **a.** Flange-necked flagon, *c.*240 on. **b.** Flanged bowl copying samian Form 38 with painted decoration, fourth century. **c.** Carinated bowl with painted decoration, fourth century. **d–f.** White ware mortaria with rim progression from second century (**d**), to early third century and beyond (**e–f**). **g.** Colour-coated mortarium with painted decoration emulating samian Form 45. **h.** Hook-rimmed bowl with painted decoration emulating samian Form 36. **i.** Carinated bowl with barbotine hunt decoration, mid fourth century. **j.** Tall, narrow-mouthed beaker with rouletted decoration, mid third century and on. (After various sources, including Keeley, Swan and Young.)

brown hue. Particularly well known are the 'hunt cups' with animal chases but some examples of phallic or erotic scenes were also in the repertoire (figure 23).

Some of the same market was also captured by the **Hadham red-slipped** wares produced at Little and Much Hadham (Hertfordshire) *c.*250–400 (see also London-Essex above) and appearing across East Anglia, the eastern Midlands and north Kent, mainly during the later fourth century (figure 8b). The red-slipped products were made alongside grey wares which seem to have been in production from the first century, but the former are regarded as diagnostic types with their distinctive orange-red-slipped dishes, bowls, and flagons with unusually narrow necks. The usual borrowing from samian forms took place but decorative styles included the occasional use of moulded and applied animal motifs. Towards the end of the fourth century the industry seems to have been one of those influenced by Saxon styles of decoration (such as triangular zones of dimples), which appear on some characteristically Roman forms such as beakers. These are known as **Romano-Saxon** types.

Nene Valley tablewares dominated the third-century market in Britain and continued to do so in the east even when they gave way to the

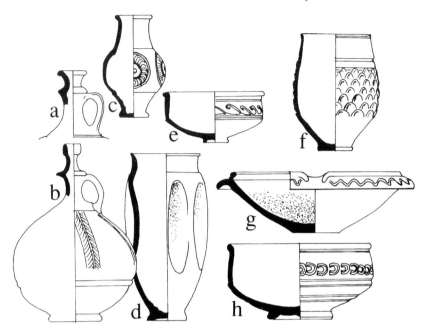

25. New Forest products *c.*260–370. Scale about 1/5. **a–b**. Flange-necked flagons. **c**. Colour-coated beaker with medallion decoration. **d**. Indented beaker (see figure 26). **e**. Carinated bowl with painted decoration. **f**. Beaker with scale decoration. **g**. Flange-rim mortarium with painted decoration in parchment ware. **h**. Carinated bowl with impressed decoration. (After various sources, including Fulford and Swan.)

26. New Forest folded and indented beaker. Late third, early fourth century. Height about 17 cm. (© Copyright the British Museum.)

Oxfordshire red- and brown-slipped tablewares in the fourth century. These were the most dominant fine wares in southern late Roman Britain, with their pre-eminence benefiting from the demise of samian, and developing from an established industry producing kitchenwares and mortaria. The range of bowls, dishes and beakers also included flagons and mortaria of higher quality than conventional kitchenware and sharing the decoration and fabric of the tablewares (figure 24). Decoration was varied and included painting, barbotine, rouletting and impressed stamps, on a range of pastel slips from orange to brown. Although samian forms, such as Forms 36, 37 and 38, were copied, no known attempt was made to produce moulded decoration. Despite the industry's importance it was typical of the period that market reach was restricted and barely impacted on the north. Nevertheless, its influence is illustrated by so-called **Pevensey** ware, which circulated between West Sussex and Hampshire using Oxfordshire forms.

New Forest tablewares were even more limited, reaching only across central southern Britain from the middle of the third century and dying out before the end of the fourth. The repertoire was the familiar combination of samian-derived bowls and dishes, 'hunt cups', beakers, flasks and flagons (figures 25, 26). Slips are mostly variations on red to reddish-brown.

5
Amphorae

Amphorae were manufactured for bulk storage and transportation. In spite of the many different types known, most were globular or cylindrical. Many were very large, often over a metre in height, with thick walls. Consequently, amphorae break into a large number of substantial sherds and make a major contribution to the dead-weight of excavated material.

With capacities from around 20 to 80 litres, amphorae were used to hold wine, oil, fish-sauce, grain, olives, seeds or other goods, and reused for innumerable secondary storage purposes. It is rare for contents to survive in any form, but their details were often marked in ink or incised on the body of the amphora. Some producers had their names stamped on the handles or necks. One from Southwark announces its contents to have been *liquamen Antipol(itanum) exc(ellens) L(uci) Tett(i)i Africani. Afri(cani)*, which means: 'Lucius Tettius Africanus's excellent fish-sauce from Antipolis [Antibes, near Nice]; (a product) of Africanus'. Occasionally, inscriptions mark ownership relating to the end-user, for example goods intended for legions, sometimes even as specific as the unit hospital, while others seem to be the property of individual soldiers, naming them, the unit and the contents.

The shapes of amphorae made for easier stacking and manhandling. Most have tapered conical bases that made it easier for them to be swung or twisted across a floor, rather than dragged, and lifted for pouring. These tapered bases, particularly on cylindrical forms, could be inserted into holes in the ground, or circular holes in wooden planks, to stack them securely. A pair of substantial handles, one on either side of the neck, was a ubiquitous and essential feature. Amphora mouths are invariably relatively small. Not only did this make pouring easier, but also it made sealing with bungs more reliable.

Amphorae arriving in Britain before the Roman conquest had usually been imported by tribal aristocrats for their contents, often being deposited in rich Iron Age graves. Dominant forms were variants on the **Dressel 1** type (figures 3, 27a) appearing in the first century BC in Essex, Cambridgeshire, north Kent and around the Solent and the Isle of Wight. The type had its origins in Italy but was also made in Gaul. It was normally used for shipping wine, sometimes for olive-oil.

During the first century AD the **Dressel 2–4** types (figures 27b, 28) were used and appear across almost all of western Europe and north Africa except central and western Spain. The basic shape is similar to the Dressel 1 but with a shorter neck which increased capacity from

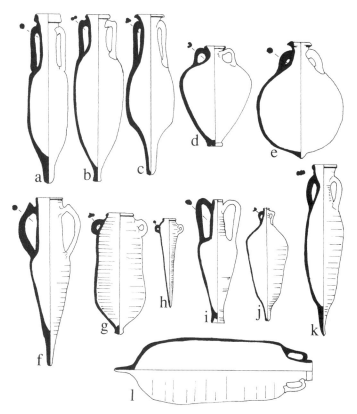

27. Amphora forms. Scale about 1/20. **a**. Dressel 1. **b**. Dressel 2–4. **c**. Dressel 7–11. **d**. Gauloise 20. **e**. Dressel 20. **f**. Rhodian. **g**. Richborough 527. **h**. *Camulodunum* 189 'carrot'. **i**. Hollow foot. **j**. British B4. **k**. London 555. **l**. North African cylindrical.

around 24 litres up to as much as 34 litres. Although predominantly continental in manufacture, some were made at **Brockley Hill**. A similar market reach was achieved by the **Dressel 7–11** forms (figure 27c), distinguished by their relatively bulbous bodies, and a tapered base reaching up to a third of the total length. These, however, are primarily associated with fish-based products.

Even more distinctive are the flat-based **Gaulish** or **Gauloise** amphorae (figure 27d). In these types the body is by far and away the principal component, with a small neck and mouth and small handles. The base is flat, like a conventional flagon or jar, but narrow. They are associated with production sites in southern Gaul but they are distributed across Britain and Gaul from the time of the conquest right through to the middle of the third century. Some of these were used for wine.

28. Amphorae. (Left) Dressel 2 from Pompeii, and thus not postdating August 79. (Right) London 555 amphora, from London, now on display at the London Museum.

During the first century wine amphorae seem mainly to have reached civilian settlements but olive-oil varieties normally dominate amphorae found at contemporary forts. The **Dressel 20** amphora (figure 27e), manufactured in southern Spain, is characterised by a substantial globular body, and a short and narrow neck with a pair of small but stout handles. However, the base was rounded and equipped with a tapered protrusion. Distribution is the same as the Dressel 2–4 types, and a typological series is recognised from the trend to more and more globular bodies and the disappearance of a more sagged lower half. The capacity, up to 80 litres, was one of the largest of all amphorae and it proved a practical and durable design used from the beginning of the first century up to the middle of the third, when it was supplanted by the smaller, but very similar, **Dressel 23**. This type is very rare in Britain, where the market seems to have been served by North African goods (see below). The so-called **London 555** amphora type (figures 27k, 28) may have come from the same area *c*.50–120 and is also scarce. One, from London, bore an inscription suggesting it had held 'twin-cluster wine' but is thought to have come from Spain.

The more exotic **Rhodian** amphorae (figure 27f) are fairly widely known in Britain from before the conquest up to *c*.150 but not in great quantities, reflecting their remote origins in the eastern Mediterranean in the Aegean and on Rhodes. Again, the main contents were wine but the source makes it likely it was perhaps a high-priced and prestige product. Pliny the Elder (*Natural History* 14.73) describes certain vintages from the Greek islands as of the 'highest esteem' amongst foreign wines. The amphorae are readily identifiable from their conical bodies, proportionately broad and long necks and distinctive handles.

Other amphorae are distinctly more restricted in their impact on the Romano-British market. The **Richborough** type resembles an open-mouthed sack apart from its handles and conical base (figure 27g). Distribution is scattered in Gaul and it appears in southern Britain normally only associated with dates from early in the first century up to *c*.230. Examples seem to have been made in Sicily presumably to ship a local, but unknown, product. The **Camulodunum carrot** types of the second half of the first century include varieties that resemble the Richborough forms (figure 27h) but are better made. Some are shaped like carrots and an inscription on one suggests it was used for palm-tree fruit, presumably from the Near East or north Africa. Examples are known thinly scattered across much of Britain.

North African cylindrical amphorae had long bulbous bodies, small necks and handles and diminutive conical bases (figure 27l). They seem to have been produced mainly for carrying olive-oil from the early second century right through the period, also being shipped into Britain on into the sixth century, with most arriving during the third and fourth centuries. They turn up mainly in London and York, the premier administrative settlements of Roman Britain, and Exeter, while other find-spots are in coastal areas or close to major river systems.

In the later part of the period, apart from the Dressel 20 and 23 types, most of the forms described had disappeared. A type known as **British B4** (figure 27j), but in fact probably from the eastern Mediterranean, has turned up scattered almost across the whole Empire in contexts associated with the third and fourth centuries. With a capacity of about 6 litres, it held only a tiny fraction of the contents of earlier amphorae. The contents (if any – it may have been sold as a container) are unknown but it is interesting that, whatever they were, the form was still arriving in Britain in minuscule quantities into the sixth century. **Hollow foot** amphorae are also considered to have an eastern origin, but the contents are unknown (figure 27i).

6
Kitchenwares

Kitchenwares, 'cooking wares' or 'coarse wares' comprise everyday pottery used for a variety of domestic and commercial purposes (figure 29). Generally they are considered to have been cheaper, less well made and more readily discarded than tablewares, apart from certain specialised products. Their remains dominate the record and even a modest excavation can generate large quantities.

Mortaria

The mortarium, or mixing bowl, is one of the most distinctive Roman ceramic products. It was rare before, and unknown after, the Roman period in Britain. The defining features are the broad bowl and substantial rim, a spout, prominent grit fragments in the bowl, and conspicuous name-stamps over the rim on some, a practice commoner in Britain than elsewhere but only during the first and second centuries (figures 31, 32). There is a distinct typological series of rims. Early imports have wall-sided rims, which progressed to prominent curved-over or hooked flanges with an internal bead in the first and early second centuries. The size of the curved flange tended to diminish during the second century while the beaded rim became more prominent. Eventually the flange and beaded rim gave way to the hammer-headed rim (figure 30).

29. Reconstructed Roman kitchen scene at the Museum of London. Note the range of black-burnished and grey-ware jars, together with the mortarium and flagon.

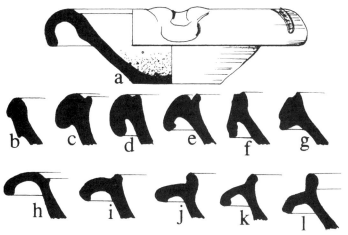

30. Mortarium types. Scale about 1/4. **a**. *Verulamium* Region, late first, early second century (but broadly similar types were made elsewhere too). **b**. Rhineland wall-sided, early to mid first century. **c**. Mayen, *c.*30–70. **d**. North Gaulish, late first century. **e**. Colchester, second century. **f**. Colchester, second century. **g**. Corbridge, second century. **h**. Lincolnshire, second century. **i**. Hartshill-Mancetter, late second century. **j**. Oxfordshire, third century. **k**. Nene Valley, third century. **l**. New Forest, late third, early fourth century.

31. Mortarium stamps (selected). VR = Brockley Hill, *Verulamium* Region; H-M = Hartshill-Mancetter. **a**. Albinus (VR), 60–90. **b**. Bruccius (VR), 80–110. **c**. Castus (Radlett), 110–40. **d**. Cillus (VR), 95–135. **e**. Doballus (Northampton), 140–80. **f**. Doinus (VR), 70–110. **g**. Driccius (VR), 100–45. **h**. Gaius Julius Pri… (North Gaul), 70–100. **i**. Lallaius/Lallans (VR), 90–130. **j**. Gaius Attius Marinus (Colchester), 90–100; (VR), 95–105; (Radlett), 100–10; (H-M), 110–30. **k**. Martinus (VR), 70–110. **l**. Matugenus (VR + H-M), 80–125. **m**. Sarrius (H-M), 135–75. **n**. Sextus Valerius C… (North Gaul), 60–90. **o**. Sollus (VR), 60–100. **p**. Quintus Valerius Veranius (North Gaul), 65–100.

32. Mortarium stamps. (Left to right) Iunius, *c.*100–40, field-walking surface find from Brockley Hill; and Doinus, *c.*70–110, from the Thames at London.

Mortaria were normally made by specialist potters. To begin with, they were imported, apparently from the **Rhineland**, probably by the army. This was where much of the British garrison had originally been based. Other imported mortaria continued to arrive throughout the first century from the **Eifel** region (lower Rhineland), **Aoste** (Central Gaul), **North Gaul**, for example those stamped by Quintus Valerius Veranius (figure 31p), and also from **Italy**. Soon after the invasion Romano-British industries developed as well. This is interesting because, as a specifically Roman product used for grinding food, the mortarium marks a change in culinary habits as well as a taste for Roman goods in general. Correspondingly, mortaria fell out of use in Britain after the Roman period.

One of the best-known sources has been identified between London and *Verulamium* (St Albans), known now as **Verulamium Region** mortaria, though other types were also made, such as flagons. Kilns and other evidence of production have been found at several places including **Radlett** and **Brockley Hill**. The latter was one of a number of potteries in the general area which developed during the middle of the first century, along with a contemporary mortarium industry at **Colchester**. Although it is impossible to say where these potters had come from, it is likely that a number moved to Britain from Gaul or Germany.

Excavations have taken place amongst the kilns of Brockley Hill. Mortaria made by many named potters have been found in and around kilns here, for example those by Doinus (active between 70 and 110, figure 32). While their dominant appearance in other sites is in the London and *Verulamium* area, mortaria made here have turned up across almost all of Britain, including Wales and the north, right into Scotland. This is useful evidence for how far manufactured products could be transported within Britain. Brockley Hill reflects the importance of access to communications, because it was on a major Roman road.

Gaius Attius Marinus's three-part name shows that he was a Roman citizen and thus a man of status when he worked in the late first and early second century. His name turns up on mortaria made at Brockley Hill (95–105), Colchester (90–100), **Hartshill-Mancetter** in Warwickshire (110–30), and Radlett in Hertfordshire (100–10) (figure 31j). The dates are approximate but he seems not to have worked at all these places at once. Either he moved around, perhaps seasonally, or he may have owned more than one concern. His name could have carried enough prestige as a manufacturer for him to subcontract work to lesser potters.

The movements of Gaius Attius Marinus can be tracked from the fabrics of his mortaria. One possibility is that his Hartshill-Mancetter base was part of a movement of like-minded mortarium potters away from the south-east. Pottery production in this area was on a major scale from *c*.100. This was also the time when legionary fortresses had been established in the north at Chester and York, and the northern frontier was being consolidated, with forts like *Vindolanda* and Corbridge being established on a line between the Tyne and the Solway Firth. Hartshill-Mancetter was well placed to serve these military markets. For example, nearly 80 per cent of second-century mortaria from the civilian settlement by the fort at Greta Bridge (North Yorkshire) was from this source (figure 33).

Urban markets in the Midlands and south were also served, though one potter called Sarrius moved further north during the second century to establish an industry at **Rossington Bridge** near Doncaster, before returning to Hartshill-Mancetter. This attention to the northern market is reflected in the development of other mortarium production centres around this time in **Lincolnshire** (at South Carlton), **Wilderspool**, and

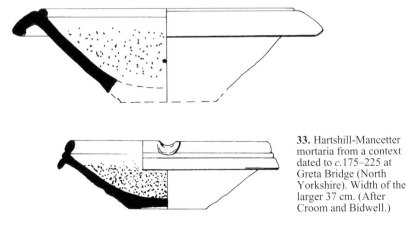

33. Hartshill-Mancetter mortaria from a context dated to *c*.175–225 at Greta Bridge (North Yorkshire). Width of the larger 37 cm. (After Croom and Bidwell.)

even on the northern frontier itself at **Corbridge** and at **Carlisle**. Several Wilderspool potters seem to have moved to the Carlisle area.

Sulloniacus was a potter based at Corbridge between about 100 and 140. *Sulloniacis* was the ancient name for Brockley Hill. Sulloniacus is not known at the latter but the possibility (purely speculative) exists that he was born there and learned his trade from his father or family before moving north to set up his own factory. This sort of family connection is certainly known at Brockley Hill where the mortarium potter Matugenus, working between 80 and 125, names himself as the son of Albinus (figure 31), active there himself between 60 and 90.

One curious variant on the second-century mortarium market was the samian mortarium, Form 45, manufactured in Central and East Gaul, and distinguished by its prominent wall-sided rim and lion's head spout with a hole far too small for practical use (figure 10r). This has given rise to the suggestion that they were decorative products, almost akin to the modern polished 'copper kettle' of antique shops. However, some were very heavily used, with one example from Billingsgate in London having a base completely worn through. But the form is not very common, and mould matches of the lion's head motif show that they were probably made by only a few potters.

Although Hartshill-Mancetter production lasted throughout the third century and well into the fourth, other early Romano-British mortaria industries declined by the end of the second century. Their share of the market was taken by imports from the **Soller** factories in the Rhineland until *c*.250 and also by mortarium potters in the **Oxfordshire** and **Nene Valley** industries. The latter two continued until the end of the period, supplemented in the fourth century by mortaria produced by the **Hadham** red-slipped industry, the **New Forest** industry, and at **Crambeck** (see below). Some Oxfordshire wall-rimmed mortaria were produced in colour-coated fine wares, resembling the samian Form 45 mortarium. Soller products seem to have found a niche market, partly because of the mortaria made by Verecundus (active *c*.150–200), which were around twice the diameter of normal examples (figure 34). Another important source from *c*.210–50 was the **Eifel-Rhine** region in Germany, where, amongst many coarse-ware products (often called **Eifelkeramik**), hammer-rim mortaria were made. The cream fabric is extremely hard, resembling stoneware, with a rough yellow-cream surface.

An exception to the anonymity of Romano-British mortaria potters of the third and fourth centuries is a painted inscription on a mortarium from the Nene Valley (figure 35). The reason name-stamping was given up may be connected with changes in marketing, with potters coming perhaps only to produce goods for bulk sale on to traders, or working for concerns owning dozens of potteries.

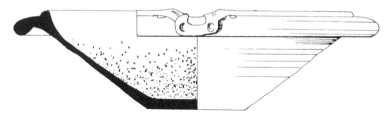

34. Specialised large mortarium by Verecundus of Soller (Germany). Diameter approximately 77 cm, plus name-stamp, diameter about 5.8 cm.

35. Painted signature on a mortarium rim from the Roman town at Water Newton (*Durobrivae*) in the Nene Valley: *Sennianus Durobrivis vri(t)*, 'Sennianus fired this at *Durobrivae*'.

Flagons

Flagons were often made in the same areas as mortaria and perhaps by the same potters. They also proliferated only after the conquest, probably because their principal use was for pouring wine. The presence of the army and the increase in imported wine will have made their widespread manufacture desirable. Certainly, the so-called 'Hofheim' types, first classified on a military site in Germany of that name, are well known from mid-first-century military sites in Britain but they made no impact on the civilian market (figure 36a). Other imported flagons include the pinch-necked form, probably imported from **north-west Gaul**. The distinctive shape was achieved by creating a wide

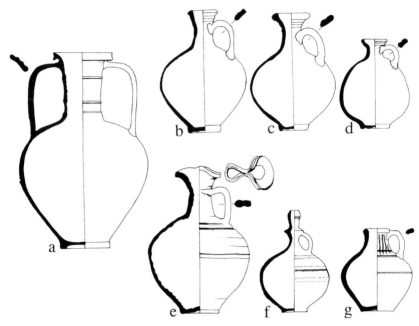

36. Flagons. Scale about 1/6. **a**. 'Hofheim' type, *c.*43–70. **b**. *Verulamium* area, *c.*70–130. **c**. *Verulamium* area, *c.*110–40. **d**. *Verulamium* area, *c.*130+. **e**. Pinch-necked flagon from north-west Gaul. **f**. Oxfordshire colour-coat, *c.*240+. **g**. Alice Holt, *c.*270+. (After Anthony, Frere, Lyne and Jefferies, Marsh and Tyers, and Swan.)

mouth and then pinching two opposite sides together to create a spout and a filler hole. Their orange-brown fabrics are often belied by a burnt-grey and rough, gritty feel to the surface (figure 36e).

By the later first century in London vast quantities of single-handled ring-necked flagons, made by **Verulamium Region white ware** potters (see below) and at **Colchester**, started to appear. They generally have cream slips, clearly conforming to contemporary fashion (figure 36b–d). These remained in production throughout the second century, most easily distinguished by the enlargement of the top ring at the expense of the others, which diminished almost to decorative features. During the third and fourth centuries flagon production seems to have become part of the repertoire of almost all the major industries including **Oxfordshire** (figures 24a, 36f), the **Nene Valley**, **Alice Holt** (figure 36g), and the **New Forest** (figure 25a–b). In these instances, flagons were frequently produced in the colour-coated ware used for other tablewares and bear rouletted or painted decoration. Some examples bear moulded faces on the necks, often with painted features.

The *Verulamium* Region white ware industry was responsible for other better-quality wheel-thrown kitchen-type products and certain specialist wares such as large double-handled flagons, face-pots, incense cups (*tazze*), lamps and carinated bowls with flat, grooved rims. They fall somewhere in between the day-to-day kitchenwares and fine wares. Like the flagons, the main period of production lasted from the mid first century to the end of the second. The industry is very well represented in London, north Kent and Essex throughout the second century but apart from scattered finds across the Midlands it never, in spite of its quality, made inroads across the rest of Britain.

German marbled wares, made in the Rhineland or along the Moselle *c*.240–350 or later, appear in very small numbers in Kent and around the Thames estuary, mainly as jugs or flagons in a range of colours from light brown through oranges and reds to dark brown. The most conspicuous diagnostic difference from earlier flagons is the much broader neck and mouth with an effect that makes them resemble the jugs of more modern times (figure 20b).

General kitchenwares

Ordinary kitchenwares are distinguished by unprepossessing grey fabrics and grey-black polished (burnished), or slipped, finishes. Their main association, like the more sophisticated mortaria and flagons, is with food and cooking (figure 29). Although this book can concentrate only on the main industries, there were innumerable short-lived local kilns serving tiny markets in urban or rural districts, such as the one found at Maidenhatch (Berkshire) in advance of motorway building. Analysis is based on fabric and form, dated by association with better-dated forms such as samian and mortaria, though the source of many still remains a mystery. While this makes kitchenwares imprecise as a chronological tool, it is also true that the lives of individual vessels were probably relatively short, making them much less likely to be residual finds. The late-first-century **Sugar Loaf Court** potter in London is, for example, known from one kiln site and a very restricted distribution of the kitchenware products. But finding such kilns is rare. More often when a new ware is identified, its source and attribution remain a mystery.

The **Black-Burnished** industries dominated the kitchenware market in the south and on the northern frontier from the second century onwards. The principal forms are broad-necked jars and a variety of dishes and bowls (figure 37), many of which were decorated with characteristic bands of cross-hatching. The industry in the south-west/Dorset area is now known as **Black-Burnished 1** and was in production throughout the period, probably developing from pre-Roman pottery production in the area, but the eventual market reach seems to have been across

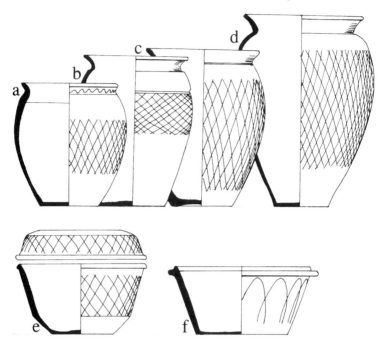

37. Black-Burnished wares. Scale about 1/5. **a.** BB1 jar, early second century. **b.** BB1 jar, late third century. **c.** BB2 jar, second century. **d.** BB2 jar, third century. **e.** BB1 flat-rimmed bowl with lid, mid second century. The angled base gradually disappears through the period. Similar products were manufactured by the BB2 industries. **f.** BB1 flanged bowl, late third to early fourth century. (After Gillam.)

Britain. Nevertheless, closer analysis of distribution by date shows that BB1 was concentrated in specific areas in the early second century, mainly London and on the northern frontier. This suggests contract purchases by official bodies and perhaps even production being supervised by Roman officials. One study has tracked BB1 finds to show movement north by road via Ilchester to the Bristol Channel, and then by sea to the north round the west coast, with other road routes north to Wroxeter and east to London.

BB1 wares were handmade, and fired in bonfires or clamps. Its attribution to the south-west is therefore by distribution and fabric analysis rather than kiln-finds. The accepted chronology today relies on a typological series. The bowl developed from one with a plain rim to a flat rim by the early second century, followed by a gradual narrowing of the base to produce a cone form and the appearance of a flange. The standard cooking pot became gradually narrower, and its everted rim became steadily more pronounced and splayed. At the same time the horizontal band of latticed decoration narrows and the angle of the intersecting lines reduces. Although the progression is not in dispute, it is unknown whether it was gradual or incremental.

A small BB1 production centre existed at **Rossington Bridge** (South Yorkshire), the products of which are also found on the Antonine Wall (active *c*.140–65). Either this was a local enterprise seeking to capture a share of the military market, or perhaps a few potters had migrated from the south-west. Difficulties with transport to more remote forts such as Ravenglass and Hardknott in Cumbria, and a lack of a local industry, may explain military pottery production of BB1-type goods at **Muncaster** in Eskdale during the first half of the second century.

By the third century BB1's reach was province-wide but in the fourth century, reflecting the regionalisation of wares, it was being supplanted in the north by local products. Some of these, such as **Knapton** ware, had been in existence from the beginning of the period. In this case, basic handmade pots circulated locally until the middle of the third century, when demand from the military frontier led to a modest expansion and improvement in the products. In the late third to early fourth century BB1-type wares were being made at **Catterick** (North Yorkshire). The products had already been identified in local assemblages before the kiln itself was found in 1994.

South Devon burnished ware was produced in the same area as BB1 but, while it seems to have lasted for much of the period, its market share was mainly confined to the southern coastal region of the south-west. A tiny amount has been found in London, which is probably due to incidental private purchases. Mostly wheel-thrown, the everted-rim jars, conical bowls and 'dog-dishes' resemble BB1 products, including the latticed decoration. The fabric can be distinguished by dark mica, which is not a feature of BB1. Clearly an acceptable alternative to BB1, this ware's limited impact shows how important other factors must have been in making BB1 so dominant.

Black-Burnished 2 pottery resembles BB1 but was manufactured in the south-east, mainly around the Thames estuary, and was more sophisticated, being wheel-thrown and kiln-fired. The products are very similar to BB1 and are dominated by everted-rim cooking jars and bowls or dog-dishes, but the industry does not seem to have started before the early second century (figure 37). Despite the more advanced manufacturing techniques, and better communications, BB2 products are mostly found only in Kent, London, Essex and Hertfordshire. However, they also turn up along the northern frontier by the end of the second century, suggesting that BB2 was also being bought up for the military market or, at any rate, was being carried north as parts of more general consignments. The fort at South Shields, for example, has produced large quantities of BB2 material in early-third-century assemblages. Indeed, BB2 may even have developed specifically to service the army trade though the industry declined during the third century. This provided the BB1 producers with a chance to fill the gap, but they were not alone.

Starting earlier than BB2, but not outliving it, was the **North Kent shell-tempered** ware industry. It seems to have been confined to producing large (40 cm high) shell-tempered storage jars in a variety of kiln sites strung out along the bleak marshes of north-west Kent beside the Thames estuary between Gravesend and Rochester. Apart from the shell fragments the fabric is often characteristically red, or red-brown to grey. These jars were evidently a specialised product, and the use of a pitch-like internal sealant suggests that they were made for shipping out local products. Salt has been suggested and, even if the substance was something else, this ware is a useful reminder that pottery movement may have been incidental to its contents, the industry being driven by an entirely different market. A modern analogy would be concentrating on the source of plastics used for supermarket milk-containers and entirely ignoring (or being ignorant of) the market in milk. These shell-tempered wares reached little further than the Thames estuary and London, perhaps because thereafter a wholesale trade split up consignments into smaller units.

The **South Midlands shell-tempered** ware seems conversely to have been traded in its own right, reaching across the Midlands and as far south as the Cotswolds, London and north Kent. A broader range of wheel-thrown, wide, undercut-rim jars, dishes and flanged bowls, decorated with a horizontal zone of narrow parallel incised lines, was produced in Bedfordshire at **Harrold**. The industry started as early as the first century but did not become significant before the fourth century, by when BB2, for instance, had dwindled. A further beneficiary of BB2's decline seems to have been **Late Roman grog-tempered** ware. Handmade, its range of everted-rim jars, flanged conical bowls, dog-dishes and crude latticed decoration obviously belongs to the Black-Burnished tradition and earned a substantial share of the market in the south-east from the late third century on.

Suppliers of the fourth-century south-east market shared it with others, for example the so-called **Portchester** wares which appear across south-eastern Britain but only during this period. Made in a variety of orange, brown and grey fabrics, the inclusion of chalk fragments is a useful defining feature as well as the forms, which are biased to wide-mouthed jars with undercut rims, and the decoration, which consisted of a zone of multiple straight horizontal lines. Flanged bowls and dog-dishes

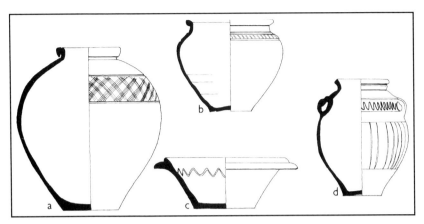

38. Alice Holt and Crambeck forms. Scale about 1/6. **a**. Alice Holt storage jar, *c*.220–70. **b**. Alice Holt cordoned jar, late first and second century. **c**. Crambeck flanged bowl, fourth century. **d**. Crambeck cordoned cooking pot, fourth century. (After Lyne and Jefferies, and Corder.)

were also produced.

The most important southern kitchenware industry operated in the **Alice Holt/Farnham** region. Although it was active throughout the period it seems to have enjoyed two boom periods: *c*.50–150, and *c*.270–380, the latter at the expense of BB2 products in London and the south-east. Compared to Black-Burnished products, Alice Holt wares are much greyer and the wide range of forms are individually better represented. But Alice Holt goods made only a minimal impact on the market outside south-eastern Britain, with only a scatter reaching as far west as the Mendips, Cotswolds and south Wales. The repertoire was extensive, including flagons (figure 36g), bowls, flanged bowls, dog-dishes and some extremely large storage jars (figures 8h, 38a–b). Zones of decoration can appear on almost any of the forms, usually as rather crude cross-hatching or wavy lines. The typological series of forms is not yet well defined for the purposes of chronology in spite of the very large quantity of surviving kilns and wasters on the kiln sites.

Kent, Essex and parts of Sussex and East Anglia were served by wares known generally as **Eifelkeramik** and **Late Roman Mayen**, made for example at Mayen, close to where the Moselle joins the Rhine. This industry, in contrast to Romano-British wares, seems to have continued until at least the tenth century. Characterised by a yellow to brown, very hard fabric, the forms include, as well as the mortaria already mentioned, jugs, cups, bowls and lid-seated jars. The last are the most common and, given the large number of Romano-British kitchenware products in the region, can probably be explained as containers for an unknown imported substance (figure 20d–e). Honey has been suggested as one possibility. Much material from this source was found in the London New Fresh Wharf deposits associated with *c*.210–50.

The kitchenware market in the Mendips, south Wales and the Welsh Marches as far north as Cheshire was served by the **Severn Valley** industry. Pottery production in the area during the first century seems to have been operated by immigrants for the army, making continental forms (figure 4) and then a conventional range of Roman kitchenwares (such as ring-necked flagons) during the second century for the civilian market. **Severn Valley ware** proper was a distinct industry whose mainly wheel-thrown products did not saturate the regional market until the second and third centuries, with scattered distribution through Lancashire, Cumbria and up to and along the Antonine Wall. The most common forms, in a characteristic orange-red and easily abraded fabric, are carinated bowls or beakers, tankards (figure 39), and a variety of conventional storage jars and pots. Some pseudo-samian forms were produced, typically emulating the Form 38 flanged bowl, and the Form 36 hook-rimmed dish (see figure 10g and p). Once more, reflecting fourth-century regionalisation, Severn Valley ware was only reaching local markets by the fourth century and not even matching the distribution scale of Alice Holt to the east.

Savernake wares, produced in Wiltshire, reached some of the same markets in the Gloucester, Bath and Cirencester area, but included a much narrower range of forms centred on a variety of wide-mouthed storage jars. Featuring a light-grey fabric with horizontal grooves around the circumference of vessels and occasionally a band of wavy-lined decoration, these products seem to have lasted in production only from the first to the early second century. There was no impact on the military

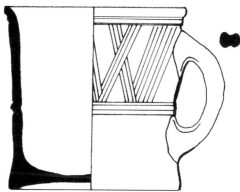

39. Severn Valley ware tankard from Kingsholm (Gloucestershire). Height about 10 cm. (After Timby.)

market, suggesting that army purchasing was a critical (but not the only) component in guaranteeing an industry's longevity.

In the later part of the period significant northern industries developed in their own right. Certainly, much of the third century was comparatively peaceful in the north. **Derbyshire** ware, confined almost entirely to the wheel-thrown bell-mouthed rim jar, was being produced at a variety of kilns in the Derby area from about 150 onwards and proceeded to dominate the immediate regional market until the third century, when it seems to have made a modest inroad across the north and the northern frontier. More significant was **Dales** ware, produced in a variety of kiln sites in Lincolnshire and Yorkshire, biased to the Humber zone. The principal product was a handmade everted-rim jar with a distinctive ridge inside the rim, and a shell-tempered grey to black or brown fabric. It began during the later second century but gained a significant market across the north, tending to the eastern parts, during the late third century and on into the fourth.

The **Crambeck** industry to the north-east of York was the most important northern pottery industry. It produced a large series of wheel-thrown forms in several distinct fabrics: grey (the dominant variety), orange-red, and white to white-yellow. Crambeck goods did not appear on the market until the fourth century. They soon became one of the most widely used wares in north-east Britain and gradually entered the north-west as well. As was typical of this period, distribution was regional and Crambeck wares are all but unknown elsewhere. The repertoire of grey wares was monopolised by handled jars (figure 38d), conical flanged bowls (figure 38c), dog-dishes, and wide-mouthed bowls with everted rims. Some pseudo-samian forms were produced in the parchment ware which resemble Form 36 dishes, while a version of the Form 38 bowl was produced in both grey and parchment wares. Parchment ware was also the favoured fabric for a variety of mortarium forms including wall-sided and hammerhead rim types. Decoration on all types was perfunctory though the parchment forms are more likely to exhibit a combination of incised lines and simple impressions of shapes.

Huntcliff wares, produced in the same region, are distinguished by their rough shell-gritted jars covering a similar area to Crambeck wares in the fourth century. Along with Knapton (see above) and other northern products they reflect a distinct division of southern and northern markets in late Roman Britain.

7
Lamps

In the Roman world fuel for lighting was supplied by the colossal Mediterranean region olive-oil industries and shipped to Britain in amphorae. Most oil lamps, *lucernae*, found in Britain were made of fired clay, though some bronze examples are known. Lamps were imported from Italy, Gaul, Germany and North Africa but some were produced in Britain, for example by the **Verulamium Region white ware** industry, at **Colchester** and in **London**. Lamps generally consist of three components: the central reservoir, the spout and the handle. The reservoir lid was pierced with a hole for filling and also to allow air to enter. It was also sometimes decorated with a design which could be anything from an image of plants to gods and goddesses, or even erotic scenes. The nozzle was usually more straightforward though volutes and curves could make it interesting (figure 40). Occasionally, more

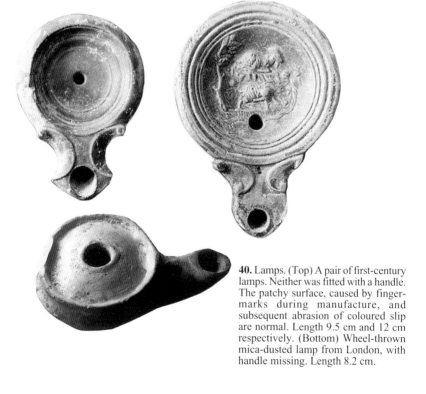

40. Lamps. (Top) A pair of first-century lamps. Neither was fitted with a handle. The patchy surface, caused by finger-marks during manufacture, and subsequent abrasion of coloured slip are normal. Length 9.5 cm and 12 cm respectively. (Bottom) Wheel-thrown mica-dusted lamp from London, with handle missing. Length 8.2 cm.

imaginative designs were used. One, from London, is a model of a sandalled foot. But others were plain and simple, some being no more than lamp-shaped open dishes.

Using a lamp meant filling it with oil, inserting a wick into the nozzle and lighting it. The result was a feeble orange light and a good deal of smoke as well as seepage of oil through the porous fabric of the pottery lamp itself (which made bronze lamps more desirable). Some of the open dishes may actually have been lamp holders. Multiple nozzles or multiple lamps produced more light but at the expense of more discomfort.

Most pottery lamps were made in moulds. A wooden or clay archetype was produced and this provided the basis for a clay or plaster mould. These generated consistent and trackable designs, and sometimes even potters' names, though diminished quality and size are probably attributable to a pirate potter using a purchased lamp as an archetype rather than bothering to make his own.

One interesting example, found in river spoil from the Thames at Billingsgate in London, is small, mica-dusted and wheel-turned (rather than moulded). It has no decoration or name-stamp but it was unused, owing to its handle having fallen off. It was therefore probably made in London itself (figure 40).

Pottery lamps are robust items and they often survive almost unscathed from antiquity. In this respect they are easier to trace and catalogue than some pottery items but they are always scarce in Britain. In practice lamps were probably not used very often except by the army and in towns. The longer evenings of the summer, unmatched elsewhere in the Empire, would have made them unnecessary while the expense of running them in long winter evenings may have been prohibitive for ordinary people. The diminishing imports in the third and fourth centuries must have restricted supplies of oil to Britain as well.

8
Graffiti and other uses of pottery

Although the function of specialised pottery forms like feeding-cups (for babies) or mortaria is fairly obvious, jars, bowls and dishes could be used for whatever was needed. However, some evidence is specific.

Graffiti
Graffiti (figure 41), and the inscriptions on amphorae discussed in Chapter 5, sometimes tell us what an individual vessel was used for. Others name the owner or are just numerals which probably refer to unspecified (and long-lost or decayed) contents. More often they are incomplete or incoherent.

Burial
During the first two centuries AD cremation was normal burial practice and Pliny the Elder observed that 'most of humanity uses pottery containers for this purpose' (*Natural History* 35.160). A typical grave includes a large everted kitchen jar containing the cremated remains, capped by a lid, or a samian dish, and accompanied by a flagon and beaker. Some vessels contained food for the deceased but the group can often be dated if the samian has a name-stamp or if a coin was included. Not only are graves the commonest sources of complete pots, but the

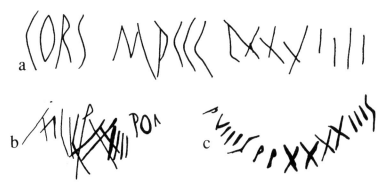

41. Graffiti on pottery. **a.** Sherd from a storage jar from *Vindolanda* marked CORS MDCCCLXXXIIII, interpreted as '1884 coriander seeds', from *cor(iandri) s(emina)*. **b.** Fragment of a storage jar from Southwark marked MEL P(ONDO) XXIIII, 'Honey, by weight, 24 [pounds]', and, in another hand, PON[DO], 'by weight'. **c.** Jug from *Vindolanda* marked [...]P VIII S P P XXXXIII S, for [*v(acuus)*] *p(ondo) (librae) viii s(emis) p(lena) p(ondo) xxxxiii s(emis)*, meaning '8½ [Roman] pounds empty, 43½ pounds full', equivalent to approximately 2.8 kg and 14.2 kg respectively. (After Frere and Tomlin.)

finding of a complete vessel like a beaker or dish may well suggest a burial even if the main container has been destroyed or decayed (especially when the remains were deposited in glass, wooden or metal containers).

Inscriptions may specify the deceased. A small bowl from a grave at Colchester containing cremated remains bears the word PVERORVM, '[remains?] of the boys', but could also mean '[property] of the boys' and refer to a previous use. A small number of face- and head-pots (figure 45) have been found in graves, but most have turned up in inconclusive deposits.

Pottery in ritual

Some pottery goods are associated with ritual. Typical of these is the *tazza* or incense cup, which normally has a conical base and carinated profile with frilled decoration around the rim and waist. Perhaps the most unusual pieces of pottery associated with ritual were the two unique clay incense burners found in a spring-head dedicated to Coventina by the fort of Carrawburgh on Hadrian's Wall. Resembling a pair of crude goblets, they were found amongst the vast cache of gifts to the goddess, which included coins and altars (figure 42).

At Lullingstone villa a small **Trier black-slipped** cup bearing the motif SVAVIS ('sweet') was deposited in a sealed cellar to accompany a pair of marble busts which were shut away there probably during the third century. The cup contained a small sheep bone, perhaps a relic of the ceremony when the chamber was sealed.

A well-known first-century flagon found in Southwark, London, bears the inscription:

42. Pottery vessel, in the form of a hollow pedestal supporting an open dish, from the spring dedicated to Covetina/ Coventina by the fort of Carrawburgh on Hadrian's Wall, inscribed COVETINA AVGVSTA VOTV(M) MANIBVS SVIS SATVRNINVS FECIT GABINIVS, 'Saturninus Gabinius made this for Covetina Augusta with his own hands'. Height 23 cm. One of a pair, probably devised as incense burners. (After Finch.)

 *Pottery in Roman Britain*

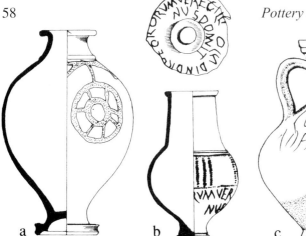

a   b   c

43. Ritual pottery (not to scale). **a**. Pottery jar with painted decoration of four wheel motifs (see figure 44). From the second-century shrine of Abandinus at Godmanchester (Cambridgeshire). Height 22 cm. (After H. Green.) **b**. Colour-coated beaker from a grave at Dunstable (Bedfordshire), with an incised inscription meaning 'Regillinus presented the pot of the *dendrophori* ['branch-bearers' associated with the worship of the eastern mother goddess Cybele] of *Verulamium*'. Height 16 cm. (After Matthews.) **c**. Late-first-century flagon from Southwark bearing a graffito: *Londinii ad fanum Isidis*, 'London, at the temple of Isis'. Height 25.4 cm.

LONDINII AD FANVM ISIDIS, 'London, at the temple of Isis' (figure 43). This probably records only an address, whereas a graffito on a colour-coated beaker from a grave at Dunstable says that it was a gift of the *dendrophori*, 'branch-bearers', of *Verulamium* (St Albans), presented by Regillinus. The *dendrophori* were associated with the cult of Cybele.

The beaker had probably come from an otherwise unknown temple at *Verulamium*. Another, from the Abandinus shrine at Godmanchester (Cambridgeshire), has painted wheels, a motif closely associated with Romano-Celtic cults (figures 43, 44).

Face- and head-pots (see

44. (Left) Impression from a mould found at Corbridge depicting a Celtic warrior god, identified as Taranis, accompanied by a wheel motif, symbolising the sun. This was used to make clay appliqué motifs for attachment to pots. Height 12 cm. (Right) The mould. Not to scale.

45. Face-pots. (Left and middle) From cremation burials in Colchester. (Right) From Lincoln (restored), bearing the painted inscription: DEO MERCVRIO, 'To the God Mercury'.

Burial above) are a special problem. One, from Lincoln, was dedicated to Mercury, but most have been found in ordinary domestic contexts and are uninscribed. They may have been used in domestic shrines, or purely as decoration (figure 45).

Coin and other hoards

In antiquity hoarding was the routine method of storing valuables, regardless of whether there was a crisis or not. Some were never recovered and these are the ones found today. Coins were usually hoarded in kitchen jars or jugs. The hoard must postdate the latest of the coins that it contains, and the container too must have been made at least by

46. The Snettisham (Norfolk) hoard. The finished jewellery, components, metal ingots and coins for melting down seem to be a jeweller's stock-in-trade. Buried in a grey vase of unknown, but probably local, origin with a manufacturing fault preventing it being watertight, perhaps sold as a 'second'. The coins date the hoard to 155+, but parallels in the jewellery mean it could have been deposited several decades later. Height of the vase 17.5 cm. (© Copyright the British Museum.)

that date. Occasionally jugs or flagons are found with slots cut into the upper wall. These are probably money-boxes, perhaps destined eventually to be shattered to recover the coins.

A remarkable instance was the pot containing the **Snettisham** (Norfolk) hoard, which comprised the work-in-progress of a jeweller of the mid second century, including not just jewellery but also a variety of silver and bronze coins, evidently selected for eventual melting down (figure 46).

Reuse and disposal of potsherds

Most potsherds were discarded without further ado. But there were other uses for them. Drilling holes made reassembling valued bowls with bronze or lead rivets possible, a surprisingly effective technique which was still in use until modern times (figure 13). Fragments were also filed down to produce circular discs used as gaming counters and spindle whorls, or cut to size to serve as mosaic tesserae. Because of its colour, samian was particularly suitable for this. In such cases, if the type or fragment is identifiable, it may help date a whole floor. The bases of broken samian cups, usually Form 33, seem to have been reused as lids, perhaps for jars (figure 10).

There may also have been a market in 'seconds'. Bowls or jugs which were either slightly distorted or not watertight owing to a flaw seem occasionally to have been used for other purposes, such as the one which served for the Snettisham hoard (figure 46). Sometimes the potters themselves held back seconds or wasters and stacked them into kilns to help protect and insulate a new batch of pots. But it is also possible that imperfect, but serviceable, vessels were marketed as cremation containers or grave goods.

In spite of these various options, most damaged or broken pots were thrown away, apart from those which were recycled (see below, page 64). At London huge quantities of samian and other fine wares were shipped in during the late first and early second century. Breakages from the voyage, or those caused during unloading, were dumped into the Thames below the wharves. This provided archaeologists with large quantities of mint assemblages, which also included 'seconds' made in London (for example figures 11, 12a, 17, 40). On all Roman sites dumped broken pot seems to have found its way into abandoned buildings, ditches, pits, gullies and earthen banks, from which archaeologists recover enormous quantities (figure 52).

9
Tiles and figurines

Fired clay was so useful a manufacturing material in the Roman world that it found many other applications besides pottery.

Tiles

Tiles were used as levelling courses in walls, to form windows, arches, and hot-air ducts in baths and heating systems, as supports for suspended floors, and for roofing (figure 47). Large, heavy and brittle, they broke easily and are found in abundance on Roman sites.

Roman tile is usually orange-red in colour with a characteristic grey core, though cream versions are also known. They were mass-produced by hand and fired in large kilns. Before firing they were laid out to dry, allowing animals and children to run across them, leaving their footprints, or other people to write comments, records or names in the wet clay. Sometimes the downward-facing side carries impressions of plants, seeds or fabrics.

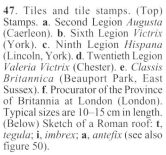

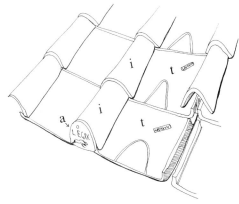

47. Tiles and tile stamps. (Top) Stamps. **a**. Second Legion *Augusta* (Caerleon). **b**. Sixth Legion *Victrix* (York). **c**. Ninth Legion *Hispana* (Lincoln, York). **d**. Twentieth Legion *Valeria Victrix* (Chester). **e**. *Classis Britannica* (Beauport Park, East Sussex). **f**. Procurator of the Province of Britannia at London (London). Typical sizes are 10–15 cm in length. (Below) Sketch of a Roman roof: **t**, *tegula*; **i**, *imbrex*; **a**, *antefix* (see also figure 50).

Being so bulky, tiles were often manufactured close to where they were to be used. At Muncaster, in the Lake District, tiles as well as pottery were made in the second century, probably for use in nearby forts. The Twentieth Legion at Chester had its own second-century pottery and tile-making depot nearby at Holt, though pottery production ceased after *c*.130–40. Legionary tiles were stamped with the legion's name, a practice adopted by most of those stationed in Britain, and some auxiliary units. This helped control production runs, and discouraged theft (figures 47, 50). Usually such tiles were used only in the unit's base but tiles of the Sixth Legion were used in the bath-house at the auxiliary frontier fort of *Vindolanda*. Occasionally, incised marks on the sides of tiles, called 'tally-marks', seem to identify the number, or batch, of tiles made. Official tiles in London were marked P P BR LON, which abbreviates the Latin for 'Procurator of the Province of Britannia at London'. At Silchester a few tiles from the public baths and the basilica name the emperor Nero (54–68), suggesting that these were provided at imperial expense.

One of the best-documented sites is the *Classis Britannica* bath-house at Beauport Park (East Sussex), which was swamped by a landslide. During excavation the remains of the stamped roof tiles were carefully gathered, and tile production for the fleet in south-east Britain analysed (figure 48). The civilian tiler Cabriabanus incorporated his name into the grooving used for mortar adherence and his work can also be tracked in Kent (figure 49). Cabriabanus's name was invisible once tiles were installed. Conversely, the *antefix* was a purely decorative feature (figures 47, 50).

Figurines and other products

Figurines were produced as a variety of moulded figures of goddesses in a white, or off-white, 'pipe-clay', typical of a number of industries in

48. Impressions on a tile from the fleet bath-house at Beauport Park (East Sussex). (Left) The normal stamp CL BR for Classis Britannica. (Right) A tile-comb, itself stamped, and used for creating grooved surfaces on tiles for mortar adherence, has been impressed into the wet clay, leaving its shape.

49. Tile with the maker's name, Cabriabanus, incorporated into the design. From Plaxtol (Kent).

the north-west provinces (figure 51). Many are identified as 'Venus' (nude standing figure) or the 'Dea Nutrix' (mother goddess, seated in a representation of a wicker chair), though figures of animals such as bulls, lions and cockerels are also known. For realism they may have been painted.

The figurines were hollow and had tiny holes drilled through the surface at discreet points to allow hot gas inside to escape during firing. Some fragments of seated goddesses are marked SERVANDUS C C A A FECIT, believed to be an abbreviation for 'Servandus made this at *Colonia Claudiae Arae Agrippinensium* [Cologne]'. Others were made in Gaul at, for example, Autun and Toulon-sur-Allier in the middle of the second century, exploiting the local white clay. They were certainly used as grave goods but may also have served in household shrines.

One particularly important assemblage is the unique group of ceramic male caricature figurines, unguent vessels in the form of animals, a

50. Antefixes (decorative terminals fixed to the ends of rows of tiles; see figure 47). (Left) The Twentieth Legion, from the legionary tilery at Holt. (Right) Portrait of Medusa, from Colchester.

51. Pipe-clay figurines. (Left) Venus figure from a riverside deposit in London. (Right) Dea Nutrix figure from Welwyn. Height of the Venus figure 15 cm. (Welwyn figure © Copyright, the British Museum.)

triple-horned bull, a figure of Hercules, and a child's bust found in a grave at Colchester with an important group of Central Gaulish lead-glazed ware, dated by coins to not long after *c*.65 (figure 7). The find, made in 1866, has proved difficult to interpret, some believing these were a child's toys, others the souvenirs of an actor's life. Another grave, at Godmanchester (Cambridgeshire), has also produced ceramic figurines, including the figure of a bull.

Clay is also an excellent medium for making moulds for casting metal. Coin-forging was quite common in the Roman world. Clay was moulded around existing coins, usually silver or gold, and then filled with base metal to produce counterfeits. But legitimate casting included the manufacture of silver and bronze spoons and other goods. At Castleford (West Yorkshire), Roman *Lagentium*, excavations produced a number of clay moulds used to cast rat-tailed spoons. Another block of fired clay, from Catterick (North Yorkshire), is thought to have been a portable clay oven known as a *clibanus*.

Considering the vast range of uses the Romans had for fired clay, it is not so surprising that they even made use of broken tiles and potsherds, *fractis testis*. In a sense they returned them to where they had come from. By grinding and mixing them with lime they could be used for pavements and thus once more became part of the ground on which the Romans walked.

10
Further reading

The published literature on Roman pottery is vast, even when considering just Britain. The following are some of the more important and/or useful pieces of work. Unfortunately, some are out of print or difficult to obtain but university libraries should have all of them. New discoveries or research are normally announced in the journal *Britannia*, published by the Society for the Promotion of Roman Studies, Senate House, Malet Street, London WC1E 7HU (telephone: 020 7862 8727; website: www.romansociety.org), and the *Journal of Roman Pottery Studies*. The Society's library is an invaluable source of this and other material.

At the time of writing, Roman pottery has found its way on to the Internet with a superb site at http://www.potsherd.uklinux.net managed by Paul Tyers. Highly recommended, it features pages on all aspects of Roman pottery together with distribution maps and illustrations. As Internet links inevitably change in time, it may be necessary to use search engines to locate this site in the future.

Anderson, A. *Interpreting Pottery*. Batsford, 1984.
de la Bédoyère, G. *Samian Ware*. Shire, 1988.
Dyson, T. (editor). *The Roman Quay at St Magnus House, London*. Special Paper Number 8 of the London and Middlesex Archaeological Society [New Fresh Wharf], 1986.
Evans, J. 'Pottery Function and Fine Wares in the Roman North', in *Journal of Roman Pottery Studies*, volume 6, 1993.
Frere, S. S., and Tomlin, R. S. O. (editors). *The Roman Inscriptions of Britain. Volume II, Fascicules 4-8*. Alan Sutton, 1994–5. (Each volume deals with various categories of marks including tile stamps, graffiti on samian and coarse pottery, and inscriptions on amphorae and other wares.)
Fulford, M. G. *New Forest Roman Pottery*. BAR (British Series) number 57, Oxford, 1975.
Hull, M. R. *The Roman Potters' Kilns of Colchester*. Research Report of the Society of Antiquaries, London, number 21, 1963.
Lyne, M. A. B., and Jefferies, R. S. *The Alice Holt / Farnham Roman Pottery Industry*. CBA Research Report Number 30, London, 1979.
Peacock, D. P. S. *Pottery in the Roman World: an Ethnoarchaeological Approach*. Longman, 1982.
Perrin, J. R. 'Roman Pottery from Excavations at and Near to the Roman Small Town of *Durobrivae*, Water Newton, Cambridgeshire, 1956–8', in *Journal of Roman Pottery Studies*, volume 8, 1999.

Rhodes, M. 'Roman Pottery Lost en Route from the Kiln to the User. A Gazetteer', in *Journal of Roman Pottery Studies*, volume 2, 1989.

Stanfield, J. A., and Simpson, G. *Central Gaulish Potters*. Oxford University Press, 1958. (Revised edition with additions published in 1990, in French, by Revue Archéologie Sites, Gonfaron.)

Swan, V. *The Pottery Kilns of Roman Britain*. RCHM Supplementary Series number 5, London, 1984.

Swan, V. 'Legio VI and Its Men: African Legionaries in Britain', in *Journal of Roman Pottery Studies*, volume 5, 1993.

Tomber, R., and Dore, J. *The National Roman Fabric Reference Collection. A Handbook*. MOLAS Monograph 2, Museum of London, 1998.

Tyers, P. *Roman Pottery in Britain*. Batsford (available via Routledge), 1996.

Webster, P. V. *Roman Samian Pottery in Britain*. CBA Practical Handbook number 13, London, 1996.

Willis, S. 'The Romanization of Pottery Assemblages during the First Century AD', in *Britannia* 27, 179ff, 1996.

Young, C. J. *Oxfordshire Roman Pottery*. BAR (British Series) Number 43, Oxford, 1979.

11
Museums

Most towns across Britain have local museum collections. These will often include Roman pottery collected from graves or kiln sites in their regions, while site museums have displays found in the town, fort or villa which they represent. The following have some of the most interesting displays, often reflecting typical local assemblages of pottery. Opening times and charges vary, so check with the institution first.

However, there is no substitute for handling Roman pottery (figure 52). For anyone interested in developing an interest in Roman ceramics, the best move is to join a local archaeological group and to help sort collections and participate in excavations. Museums will usually have details but another invaluable source of up-to-date information is the magazine *Current Archaeology*, available by subscription from 9 Nassington Road, London NW3 2TX (telephone: 08456 44 77 07; website: www.archaeology.co.uk).

Ashmolean Museum of Art and Archaeology, Beaumont Street, Oxford OX1 2PH. Telephone: 01865 278000. Website: www.ashmol.ox.ac.uk

British Museum, Great Russell Street, London WC1B 3DG. Telephone: 020 7323 8299. Website: www.thebritishmuseum.ac.uk

52. Pottery processing. Pottery from the excavation of a Roman villa site at Lower Basildon (Berkshire) is processed on site. Cleaning and sorting pottery like this is the ideal way to become familiar with fabrics, forms and types.

Canterbury Roman Museum, Butchery Lane, Canterbury, Kent CT1 2JR. Telephone: 01227 785575. Website: www.canterbury.co.uk

Castle Museum, Castle Park, Colchester, Essex CO1 1TJ. Telephone: 01206 282939. Website: www.colchestermuseums.org.uk Finds include the remarkable material from the Colchester samian industry.

Corbridge Roman Site Museum, Corbridge, Northumberland NE45 5NT. Telephone: 01434 632349. Website: www.english-heritage.org.uk

Corinium Museum, Park Street, Cirencester, Gloucestershire GL7 2BX. Telephone: 01285 655611. Website: www.cotswold.gov.uk/museum

Museum of London, London Wall, London EC2Y 5HN. Telephone: 020 7600 3699. Website: www.museumoflondon.org.uk

Norwich Castle Museum, The Castle, Norwich, Norfolk NR1 3JU. Telephone: 01603 493625. Website: www.museums.norfolk.gov.uk

Peterborough City Museum and Art Gallery, Priestgate, Peterborough, Cambridgeshire PE1 1LF. Telephone: 01733 343329. Website: www.peterboroughheritage.org.uk

Rochester Guildhall Museum, High Street, Rochester, Kent ME1 1PY. Telephone: 01634 848717. Website: www.medway.gov.uk

Roman Legionary Museum, High Street, Caerleon, Newport, South Wales NP6 1AE. Telephone: 01633 423134. Website: www.nmgw.ac.uk

South Shields Arbeia Roman Fort, Baring Street, South Shields, Tyne and Wear NE33 2BB. Telephone: 0191 456 1369. Website: www.twmuseums.org.uk/arbeia

Tullie House Museum and Art Gallery, Castle Street, Carlisle, Cumbria CA3 8TP. Telephone: 01228 534781. Website: www.tulliehouse.co.uk

Verulamium Museum, St Michael's Street, St Albans, Hertfordshire AL3 4SW. Telephone: 01727 751810. Website: www.stalbansmuseums.org.uk

Vindolanda Roman Fort Museum, Chesterholm Museum, Bardon Mill, Hexham, Northumberland NE47 7JN. Telephone: 01434 344277. Website: www.vindolanda.com

Yorkshire Museum, Museum Gardens, York YO1 7FR. Telephone: 01904 687687. Website: www.yorkshiremuseum.org.uk

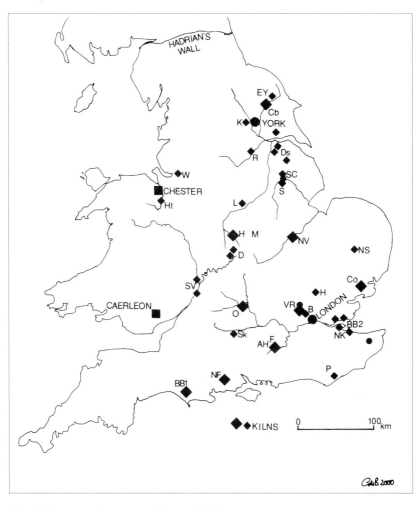

Map 1. Pottery production sites in Roman Britain.
AH/F = Alice Holt/Farnham. B = Brockley Hill. BB1 = South Dorset, Black-Burnished 1.
BB2 = Black-Burnished 2 (including Upchurch, Higham). Cb = Crambeck. Co = Colchester.
D = Derbyshire. Ds = Dales. EY = East Yorkshire. H = Hadham. H-M = Hartshill-Mancetter.
Ht = Holt. K = Knapton. L = Littlechester. NF = New Forest. NK = North Kent. NS = North
Suffolk. NV = Nene Valley. O = Oxfordshire. P = Pevensey. R = Rossington. S = Swanpool.
SC = South Carlton. Sk = Savernake. SV = Severn Valley. VR = Verulamium Region
(including Radlett). W = Wilderspool. The principal legionary fortresses are also marked at
Chester, Caerleon and the fortress-colony at York.

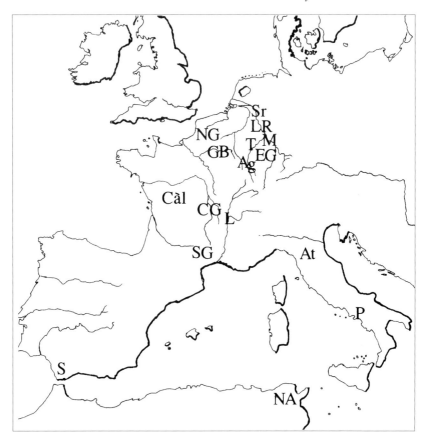

Map 2. Main sources of imported pottery.
Ag = Argonne ware. At = Arretine ware. Càl = *Céramique à l'éponge*. CG = Central Gaulish black-slipped ware, colour-coated, glazed, micaceous and samian. EG = East Gaulish samian. GB = Gallo-Belgic wares. L = Lyon ware. LR = Lower Rhineland (Cologne) colour-coated ware. M = Late Roman Mayen ware (*Eifelkeramik*). NA = North African red slip ware. NG = North Gaul grey ware. P = Pompeian red (also from the CG area). S = Spanish colour-coated ware. SG = South Gaul. Sr = Soller mortaria. T = Trier black-slipped ware.

Index

Page numbers in italic refer to illustrations.

Pottery in Roman Britain